Creativity and Constraint

INTRAC NGO Management and Policy Series

1. *Institutional Development and NGOs in Africa: Policy Perspectives for European Development Agencies* Alan Fowler with Piers Campbell and Brian Pratt

2. *Governance, Democracy and Conditionality: What Role for NGOs?* Edited by Andrew Clayton

3. *Measuring the Process: Guidelines for Evaluating Social Development* David Marsden, Peter Oakley and Brian Pratt

4. *Strengthening the Capacity of NGOs: Cases of Small Enterprise Development Agencies in Africa* Caroline Sahley

5. *NGOs, Civil Society and the State: Building Democracy in Transitional Countries* Edited by Andrew Clayton

6. *Outcomes and Impact: Evaluating Change in Social Development* Peter Oakley, Brian Pratt and Andrew Clayton

7. *Demystifying Organisation Development: Practical Capacity Building Experiences of African NGOs* Rick James

8. *Direct Funding from a Southern Perspective: Strengthening Civil Society?* INTRAC

9. *NGO Responses to Urban Poverty: Service Providers or Partners in Planning?* Caroline Sahley and Brian Pratt

10. *Financial Management for Development: Accounting and Finance for the Non-specialist in Development Organisations* John Cammack

11. *NGOs Engaging with Business: A World of Difference and a Difference to the World* Simon Heap

12. *Power and Partnership? Experiences of NGO Capacity-Building* Edited by Rick James

13. *Evaluating Empowerment: Reviewing the Concept and Practice* Edited by Peter Oakley

14. *Knowledge, Power and Development Agendas: NGOs North and South* Emma Mawdsley, Janet Townsend, Gina Porter and Peter Oakley

15. *People and Change: Exploring Capacity-Building in NGOs* Rick James

16. *Changing Expectations?: The Concept and Practice of Civil Society in International Development* INTRAC

17. *The Development of Civil Society in Central Asia* Edited by Janice Giffen and Simon Heap

18. *Creativity and Constraint: Grass-roots Monitoring and Evaluation and the International Aid Arena* Edited by Lucy Earle

Creativity and Constraint

Grass-roots Monitoring and Evaluation and the International Aid Arena

Edited by Lucy Earle

INTRAC NGO Management and Policy Series No. 18

An INTRAC Publication

INTRAC:

A Summary Description
INTRAC, the International NGO Training and Research Centre, was set up in 1991 to provide specially designed training, consultancy and research services to organisations involved in international development and relief. Our goal is to improve NGO performance by exploring policy issues and by strengthening management and organisational effectiveness.

First published in 2004 in the UK by
INTRAC
PO Box 563
Oxford
OX2 6RZ
United Kingdom

Tel: +44 (0)1865 201851
Fax: +44 (0)1865 201852
e-mail: info@intrac.org
website: www.intrac.org

ISBN 1-897748-81-7

Designed and produced by
Jerry Burman
Tel: +44 (0)1803 409754

Printed in Great Britain by
Antony Rowe Ltd., Chippenham, Wiltshire

Dedicated to Ceri Angood, Conference Organiser, for her professionalism and sense of humour that made the conference such a success.

Contents

Foreword

Brian Pratt

INTRAC's Fifth Conference on the Evaluation of Social Development[1] set out to tackle the apparent increasing polarisation between managerial monitoring and evaluation systems that owe their origins to the private and military sectors, and more participatory approaches that place their emphasis on clients' knowledge and perceptions of change. At the planning stage of the conference, the steering group felt that there were three key areas that should be explored further at the conference.

The first of these was the apparent 'rediscovery' of the need for improved monitoring. It is difficult, to say the least, to assess impact without monitoring, although there have been several systematic attempts at this. These have always run into problems, however, since it is difficult to know what changes occurred during the life of a programme or process, and problematic to assume that people's memory of these changes is accurate. Now, in contrast, there is a trend towards the use of performance assessment and measurement as a tool with which to undertake monitoring. It was therefore our intention to examine this trend during the course of the conference.

The second issue was one that had been emerging ever more frequently in the course of INTRAC's work: the inherent tension between, on the one hand, formal monitoring and evaluation (M&E) systems often introduced by donor agencies, which stress outputs and activities (as symbolised in the now ubiquitous logical frameworks or logframes) and on the other hand, the need to assess impact. The latter, we feel, involves moving beyond the measurement of outputs, to the assessment of *change*. The evidence seems to show that this can only be done with a mixture of both qualitative and quantitative methods. It also follows that if change is our key focus, we must ask ourselves whose definition of change we are using. This definition could reflect the views of a distant donor, a programme director, an external academic evaluator, or, indeed, those of key stakeholders.

Finally, it was considered important to examine the move to client-based M&E systems, as one of the most exciting innovations of recent years. This development has come about as a result of concurrence between those who stress the importance of participation and those who feel we should use a 'free market' type of analysis which privileges a demand-based system of development. The latter approach would favour the poor having a voice in determining the types of development intervention aimed at them, rather than just being beneficiaries of whatever they

---

[1] See the Appendix for a review of the findings of the four previous conferences.

are lucky enough to find coming their way. In the wider arena, this move from supply to demand-led development can also be linked to changes in the value placed on civil society groups, and on participation, transparency, accountability and democratisation.

One of the main challenges of the Fifth Conference revolved around the question of reconciling the need for client-based learning and accountability with requirements for upwards accountability to donors and treasuries, or even if these two different approaches could be reconciled at all. Top-down performance measurement systems are often tied to bureaucratic demands for accountability and efficiency, rather than a desire to ensure maximum impact for clients or 'primary stakeholders'.

To focus our attention on these issues, we commissioned two contrasting papers. The first was a review of the history and development of performance appraisal systems, based on a review of the management literature and the origins and practice of different approaches. This paper was presented by John Hailey.[2] A second, more conceptual paper, by David Marsden (Chapter 3 of this volume) reflected on the changing nature of the concepts underlying development assistance and hence its monitoring and evaluation. The participants were encouraged to review the issues presented in plenary and panel sessions in discussion groups. Halfway through the conference we opened the floor to all participants, giving them the opportunity to tell their stories in smaller groups and feedback to plenary.

The success of the conference was largely due to the participation and energy of those who attended. It was, to date, the most well attended in this series of conferences, with a great diversity of participants from nearly forty countries. Over one third of attendees were based in the South, and those from the North were from a range of NGOs, donor and bi-lateral agencies. We were also lucky to count upon a large number of insightful contributions to panel sessions. Versions of some of these are included in this volume and all of them have influenced the thinking behind this publication.

---

[2] Hailey and Sorgenfrei 2004.

Acknowledgements

INTRAC is very grateful to the conference steering group, whose members helped to shape the agenda as well as provide valuable support during the conference itself. They are Yvonne Es (Novib), Ronald Lucardie (Cordaid), Janet Townsend (University of Durham and INTRAC Board member), and Howard Dalzell and Connell Foley (Concern Worldwide). We would also like to thank INTRAC staff members Jerry Adams, Anne Garbutt and Brenda Lipson for their contributions and facilitation assistance. Special thanks go out to Rhonda Chapman from ACFID for her help planning and facilitating activities on the fourth day of the conference.

The conference was held at Kontakt der Kontinenten, Amersfoort, The Netherlands and we are grateful to the attentive staff who provided a supportive environment for all participants. The free loan of bicycles was also greatly appreciated.

In terms of financial support, the conference would not have been possible without the generosity of the Dutch Foreign Ministry, the Evaluation Department of DFID, Cordaid, Concern, DanChurchAid and Norwegian Church Aid. A number of participants were sponsored by individual agencies, for which we are grateful.

The overall conference organiser was Ceri Angood, who arranged the proceedings single-handedly and did an outstanding job.

Finally, we would like to extend thanks to Oliver Bakewell and Jonathan Benthall who read the manuscript of this volume prior to its publication and provided insightful comments, and to Jacqueline Smith who copy-edited the final script.

Notes on Contributors

Jennifer Chapman works at ActionAid in the Impact Assessment unit as project coordinator for an action research initiative with country programmes and partners in Brazil, Ghana, Nepal and Uganda. The project aims to develop innovative methodologies for assessing the impact of advocacy work.

Sadhvi Dar is a Ph.D. candidate at the Judge Institute of Management Studies at the University of Cambridge. She has recently conducted fieldwork in India for her thesis, which focuses on management issues within international NGOs.

Rosalind David is an independent consultant based in Auckland, New Zealand. At the time her contribution to this publication was written she was working at ActionAid, where she helped design and draft the initial ideas behind ActionAid's Accountability, Learning and Planning System (ALPS).

Lucy Earle is a researcher at INTRAC. She joined in 2002 and has been closely involved with INTRAC's Central Asia programme as well as the organisation's series of conferences on monitoring and evaluation and on civil society.

Antonella Mancini has worked at ActionAid for over ten years and is currently Head of Impact Assessment. Recently she has supported the introduction of ActionAid's new Accountability Learning and Planning System (ALPS) into country programmes.

David Marsden is lead social development specialist for the South Asia region in the World Bank and is based in Washington. He is an INTRAC associate and former INTRAC research director.

Peter Morgan is an independent consultant in Washington DC and is a member of the Praxis Advisory Committee within INTRAC. He is also a member of a research team in the European Center for Development Policy Management (ECDPM) which is conducting a study for the Development Assistance Committee of the OECD on capacity, change and performance.

Yedla Padmavathi is zonal director of Save the Children UK's India South Zone. Since joining the organisation in 2000 she has worked to incorporate children fully into internal processes of design, monitoring and evaluation of projects.

Brian Pratt is INTRAC Executive Director and one of the organisation's founding members. His recent publications and consultancies have principally focused on strategic policy issues for NGOs, and on monitoring and evaluation.

Peter Sigsgaard has worked at MS Denmark for over twenty years. He has held a number of overseas posts but is now based in Copenhagen as a programme coordinator. He is closely involved with the East Africa region and works on programme development and monitoring and evaluation.

Sue Soal has worked in development since 1989 and is at present a practitioner with the Community Development Resource Association (CDRA) in Cape Town, South Africa, which she joined in 1994. She is particularly interested in organisational learning processes and their connection to field practice and its evaluation.

James Taylor has been a development practitioner since 1977 and is at present the director of the Community Development Resource Association (CDRA) in Cape Town, South Africa, where he has worked since 1992. He has a special interest in exploring practical ways for complex delivery systems to become more effective in providing truly developmental and empowering services.

Tina Wallace has worked extensively on both research and practice in development agencies and at universities in the UK and Africa. She is currently completing a three country study on aid and its implications for promoting local development.

Acronyms

AA	ActionAid
AAI	ActionAid India
ACFOA	Australian Council for Overseas Aid
ACFID	Australian Council for International Development
ACORD	Agency for Co-operation and Research and Development
AIDS	Acquired Immuno Deficiency Syndrome
ALPS	Accounting, Learning, and Planning System
AusAid	Australian Agency for International Development
BOAG	British Overseas Agencies Group
CAFOD	Catholic Agency for Overseas Development
CARE	Co-operative for Assistance and Relief Everywhere
CBO	Community-Based Organisation
CDRA	Community Development Research Association
CDRN	Community Development Research Network
CIDA	Canadian International Development Agency
CNN	Christian News Network
CSCF	Civil Society Challenge Fund
CSP	Country Strategy Paper
DA	Development Area
DAC	Development Assistance Committee
Danida	Danish International Development Agency
DFID	Department for International Development
DOMINGO	Directors of Medium-Sized Non-Governmental Organisations
EC	European Community
ESCOR	Economic and Social Council Resolution
EU	European Union
GEF	Global Environment Facility
HIV/AIDS	Human Immunodeficiency Virus/Acquired Immuno Deficiency Syndrome
HQ	Headquarters
IEC	Information, Education, and Communication
INGO	International Non-Governmental Organisation
INTRAC	International NGO Training and Research Centre
LFA	Logical Framework Approach
M&E	Monitoring and Evaluation
MDG	Millennium Development Goal
MIS	Management Information System

MISR	Makerere Institute for Social Research
MRO	Mandal Revenue Officer
MS	Mellemfolkeligt Samvirke
MSC	Most Significant Change
MSM	Men who have Sex with Men
NGO	Non-Governmental Organisation
ODA	Overseas Development Assistance
OECD	Organisation of Economic Cooperation and Development
OVI	objectively verifiable indicators
PAB	Police Advisory Board
PARC	Performance Assessment Resource Centre
PCM	Project Cycle Management
PLA	Participatory Learning and Action
PPA	programme partnership agreement
PRA	Participatory Rural Appraisal
PRRP	Participatory Review and Reflection Process
PRSP	Poverty Reduction Strategy Papers
SCF	Save the Children Fund
SCUK	Save the Children – United Kingdom
SMART	Specific Measurable Attainable Realistic Tangible
SOS Sahel	SOS Sahel International – United Kingdom
STD	Sexually Transmitted Disease
SWOT	Strength Weakness Opportunity Threat
UK NGO	United Kingdom Non-Governmental Organisation
UNAIDS	Joint United Nations Programme on HIV/AIDS
UNCTAD	United Nations Conference on Trade and Development
UNDP	United Nations Development Programme
UN ESCOR	United Nations Economic and Social Council Resolution
UNICEF	United Nations Children's Fund
VSO	Voluntary Service Overseas
WHO	World Health Organisation

Introduction

Lucy Earle – INTRAC

INTRAC's Fifth International Conference on the Evaluation of Social Development, held in April 2003 in the Netherlands, brought together 120 participants from 40 countries. Over five days participants heard papers in plenary and themed workshops sessions, and were involved in discussion groups that encouraged debate and reflection at the end of each day. Levels of interest were maintained throughout by the high standard of keynote presentations, but perhaps the lasting memory of the conference for participants will be the enthusiasm and energy created by the fourth day's 'buzz group' session. This day had purposefully been left unplanned on the agenda, so as to be able to respond to the dynamics of participants' discussions and interests after three days of immersion in the topic of monitoring and evaluation (M&E). On this fourth day, participants were encouraged to share positive experiences of M&E in groups of about ten people. The enthusiasm generated by accounts of creative, alternative ways to assess progress towards organisational and project goals was remarkable. Groups carried on 'buzzing' into break times and after the end of the conference day. Participants were obviously eager to glean as much information as possible from each other about their personal experiences with M&E in the field.

There was a similar response to the keynote speech by Yedla Padmavathi from Save the Children UK's India South Zone. Illustrated with vivid photography, she gave an insight into the creative and challenging process of M&E involving children fully at every stage. Here was an example of a practitioner ensuring that her M&E practice matched the rhetoric of the organization she worked for. It became clear, after the presentation, that participants wanted and needed to hear about more such experiences of innovative practice at the grass roots, and this led us to plan the buzz group sessions.

Why did these two sessions generate so much energy and excitement? For so many in the development sector, contact with the evaluation process is limited to the reading of dry reports that have been rewritten and reworked to fit donor agendas. In contrast, the informal presentations participants made to their buzz groups were vivid and immediate and brought out fully the nuances and specificity of local contexts. Furthermore, (unlike, unfortunately, during most of the conference) those doing most of the talking were fieldworkers from the South. For office-bound Northern participants, this was a window into the real world of development. For other Southern participants, these were examples of innovative, and even daring, practice that could perhaps have resonance for their own work. So often the question raised was 'how did you manage this?', meaning, 'how did you get around institutional constraints to have it your way and do something different?'.

It could be argued that the conference had moved away from its original premise: to facilitate discussion of the tension between top-down performance-based management and client-based participatory M&E. This tension, between results-based management systems on the one hand, and responsive, reflective and participatory approaches on the other, is a very real one, played out for many in the sector on a daily basis. The opportunity to discuss the nature of this tension, to debate whether these two approaches are indeed mutually exclusive, contradictory even, or to investigate the nature of a compromise, was presumably what brought the participants to the Netherlands in the first place. We were introduced to the concept of results-based management by John Hailey and Mia Sorgenfrei on the first day of proceedings, through a thorough examination and analysis of the history of various measurement systems. This showed a parallel evolution of the practice of M&E in the business, public and non-profit sectors. But whilst this paper concluded that, 'the key is not the choice of framework, but how it is applied',[1] discussions over the following days showed a widespread unease with the continued use of some of these frameworks. Indeed, in one dramatic presentation, a 'logframe' was symbolically ripped up, to widespread applause. Here, very definitely, the message was, 'these tools do not work for us, and we do not want to be forced to use them'. This is not to suggest that we do not need measurement: Taylor and Soal argue in Chapter 5 that we all measure, all the time, in every aspect of our lives and then take decisions based on these measurements. However, it is the rigidity of certain management frameworks that causes so many problems for development sector workers.

Rather than discuss the use of results-based management systems, if anything, participants seemed reluctant to engage with the topic. Whilst there were some suggestions that the use of the logframe was an important issue for debate, it failed to capture the imagination of participants. Of course, donor insistence on its use, and its widespread application would have made it a highly relevant topic for the conference, and yet it does seem as though arguments for and against the use of the logframe have been rehearsed ad nauseam. Although one participant from a European bi-lateral agency stated, 'We want to be part of the solution, not part of the problem', the conference seemed to turn its back on a search for compromise, in favour of an exploration of the ways in which those at the frontline of the development process have managed to reject or manipulate hierarchically imposed frameworks. There was a feeling amongst some participants that if after years of use people are still struggling with tools (such as the logframe) that advocate a mechanistic approach to planning, implementing and assessing activities, it is perhaps time to reject these outright and search for more flexible methods. Whilst not all of those present were so radical in approach, in general there was an emerging

---

[1] Hailey and Sorgenfrei (2004).

consensus that development work is fundamentally constrained by the way in which the aid sector functions and that these constraints are closely tied to the practice of M&E.

The perceived institutional barriers to innovative practice in M&E led much debate at the conference in the direction of an 'us versus them' dichotomy: those higher up the aid chain were seen as responsible for the problems lower down. Furthermore, the conference focus on reporting and monitoring opened up space for a more general discussion of malaise amongst development sector workers. This is not surprising, as the practice of M&E is indivisible from the shape of the sector as a whole. As M&E is designed to assess everything that an organisation has been doing, it uncovers problems, opens wounds and tends to make people defensive, at all levels of the aid chain. Importantly, reporting is generally the main point of contact between donors in the North and practitioners in the South. In an ideal world, this could be an opportunity for dialogue, learning and negotiation. As it stands, it tends to be a tense, and sometimes dishonest process, where top-down directives intimidate Southern 'partners' and overshadow innovative local approaches. The whole process of reporting can therefore often serve, inadvertently, to highlight gross imbalances of power within the system, and expose the clash between different ways of working.

Indeed, the frustration that many practitioners feel at being compelled to operate in a certain way found voice in one of the most frequently used arguments in papers submitted to the conference. This centred around the nature of change and its lack of fit with rigorous planning and monitoring frameworks. Statements regarding non-linearity, unpredictability, unexpected outcomes and even chaos have been repeated so often as to have become truisms. For example, on the final day of the conference, one participant summed up his impression of discussions at the conference with a series of graphs. His presentation was a light-hearted résumé but, at a different level, was also illustrative of the static nature of debate around measurement of development outcomes: none of the figures below really require much explanation. For those in the sector, these arguments have been repeated so often as to have become almost instantly recognisable, even in graphic form.

Fig 1:
The processes that unfold as a result of project activities are often unpredictable, and the state of affairs at local level will be affected by external events and other inputs. Attempting to plot a strict trajectory from input to outcome will therefore be beset by almost insurmountable difficulties.

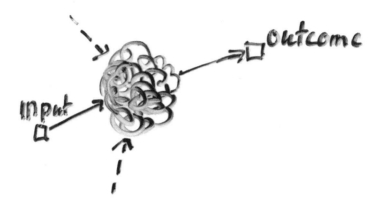

Fig 2:
It is sometimes the case that projects receive funding for many years without any significant results and it is only after ten years or more that important outcomes become visible. As such, monitoring of progress after only three years will very likely produce a negative picture of what is potentially a successful intervention.

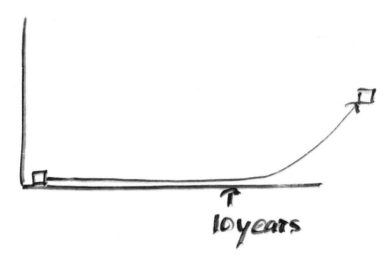

Fig 3:
Very often a large number of different, small-scale activities are carried out in the pursuit of an overarching goal. It is clear that many of these may fail, whilst one or two might exceed expectations. It is almost impossible to predict which activities will be effective.

Fig 4:
Development projects will always have a planned final result. However, unintended effects, both positive and negative, can be much more significant than the planned eventual outcome.

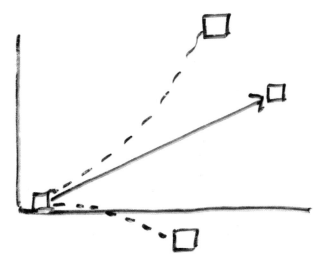

What is surprising here is that people from such different levels and areas of the development sector were repeating the same arguments and voicing the same complaints (the creator of these graphs works within a European bi-lateral aid agency). It is unlikely that anyone would challenge strongly this participant's trajectories of the life of most development projects. Similarly, few would argue against the importance of the client or beneficiary in project planning, monitoring and evaluation. And yet it would appear that these arguments have been repeated over and over for years, without any notable alteration to donor policy that might mitigate some of the problems caused by, for example, demands for short-term interventions and early reporting on impact. It is not as though nobody were listening to these repeated arguments, but unfortunately, those who could promote change, in general, cannot or will not attempt to push through different ways of working.

This book attempts to understand why individuals and organisations in the development sector are experiencing feelings of constriction and, as a consequence, the desire for rebellion. It aims to encapsulate key points of the debate heard at the conference as well as open up some of these debates to further scrutiny. The majority of papers in this volume were presented as first drafts either in plenary or in workshop sessions. They introduce the reader to current attitudes towards funding, monitoring and reporting in the development sector and analyse the problems inherent in organisational processes that are commonly guided by mechanistic or audit-driven approaches. They also suggest some innovative ways out of the perceived impasse that prevents those at the grass roots from reacting in creative ways to the problems they are addressing. The book is divided into two sections: the first contains more theoretical contributions, whilst the second provides case studies of attempts, within development organisations, to change the way in which M&E is carried out. In general, all of these contributions in this eclectic collection show that attempts to challenge accepted ways of working and to subvert hierarchies and standard practice are not without serious obstacles.

An example of the type of problem faced by practitioners who attempt to incorporate the voice of clients/beneficiaries into their monitoring and reporting even became apparent during the conference proceedings. Whilst the activities of the buzz group session on the fourth day were uplifting and inspirational, the eventual output of the session was strangely disappointing. In a way, it mirrored what happens in the reporting chain itself. Whenever a buzz group felt ready, one story that had been shared within it was presented to all the other groups in the room. In order to prevent speakers from overrunning, the person who had originally told the story in the group could not be the one to present it in plenary. A separate panel was also in place to take notes from the stories and pull out the main 'lessons learned' from the M&E experience. However, as the stories were mediated through others and then interpreted by individuals who had not heard the original version, so they lost their colour and immediacy. We were left with a list of platitudes and startlingly obvious observations. In a previous workshop session, James Taylor had used the metaphor of a funnel to describe a typical reporting process: colourful experiences are fed into the funnel but what emerges at the end is a 'grey mush'. The same could be said for the outcome of this particular session.

What was special about the buzz group session and what made it so highly valued by participants, was the space it gave for 'voices' from the front line of development interventions. This search for 'authenticity' is reflected in a number of newer approaches to the gathering of data for monitoring and evaluation purposes. One such approach discussed during the conference was the 'Most Significant Change' methodology, described in more detail by Peter Sigsgaard in Chapter 7. In the original methodology, developed by Rick Davies, informants are requested to speak about the changes they have witnessed in their own lives. In this case, subjectivity is valued as informants are required to state which had been the most significant of all these changes. The stories are recorded but not altered. As they rise up through the aid chain, the number of stories is reduced as staff at different levels of management select those they consider most important or, indeed, significant. This search for the unmediated voice is also apparent in the work of other sociologists. For example, Hulme has discussed the merits of life histories, as a way to gain real understanding of what it means to be poor.[2]

The starting point for **Yedla Padmavathi**'s work on assessing progress against Save the Children goals in its India South Zone is also narrative. Children in difficult or disadvantaged situations are interviewed and encouraged to speak about their dreams and disadvantages. Case studies are then drawn up from these accounts, and other children review these in order to establish a benchmark and to set future standards and indicators for their own lives, their families and villages. Children involved in project activities are then brought together to assess progress towards these goals. Although there are risks involved in children's intensive participation in review exercises that take them away from home and school, there is a sense that the amount of learning generated by these processes is huge, both for the children and for the organisation. Quite remarkably, children very often have the last word in internal discussions and decision-making in the SCUK South Zone, to the extent that they can veto staff choice of new appointments. The dominance of children's voices in the project came across in the use of quotations in her keynote address as well as the paper published here as Chapter 6.

Moving towards a more theoretical approach to similar issues, **David Marsden**'s paper takes on the theme of 'disembodied knowledge' and the tendency within the development sector to try to understand the world by controlling knowledge. His paper provides an analysis of a series of metaphors through which

---

[2] Hulme (2003).

15

those involved in development have viewed the world over the past decades. Rejecting the machine-age focus on predictability and efficiency, Marsden argues that the metaphor of organisation as a complex living organism can give greater insight into the way in which individuals and groups interact. Chapter 3 should be read as a reflection on the attempts of the author, who has bridged the gap between academia and development practice, to introduce greater levels of cultural and contextual awareness into the World Bank, where he is now based.

The problem of how we mediate knowledge and information is also addressed by **Sadhvi Dar** in her contribution to this volume (Chapter 4). Focusing on reporting as an integral part of development practice, she shows how the use of language in reports can create organisational identity, and skirt around difficult issues of for example, participation, by presenting a convincing image of participatory practice. This, she argues, is leading to a homogenisation of development practice, as those who write reports adopt standard, 'ceremonial' practices (which are not necessarily appropriate or efficient) developed in the North, and concentrate on shared activities and common goals. As such, a report can gloss over much of the local context. Organisations may alter their image through a re-labelling process, but the nature of relationships between North and South mean that changes in practice are rarely forthcoming. Dar's chapter ends with a fascinating analysis of an annual report, in which she shows how accounts of client behaviour can be manipulated and used to reconfirm gender stereotypes and to institutionalise particular ways of working.

MS Denmark's laudable attempt to record 'voices' and priorities of clients through the 'Most Significant Change' (MSC) methodology stands in contrast to the anonymous yet powerful author of the report analysed by Dar. However, as **Peter Sigsgaard** shows in Chapter 7, it is harder to get an authentic 'story' than might be imagined. As he notes, informants in the field are now so used to development jargon that merely speaking their minds about change has become difficult. Instead, staff members taking part in the pilot of the methodology sometimes offered researchers a logframe, saying they would then think up a 'story' to fit around it. They were unwilling or unable to talk about changes in the project area without couching it in terms of a 'logical' progression from input to outcome. Also more complexly, MS itself chose to mediate the voices of clients and beneficiaries, by asking field staff to say what they thought were the most significant changes in the lives of poorer people. The paper gives details of some of the obstacles the author and his colleagues faced in attempting to push through this new way of working. Teething problems aside, overall, Sigsgaard sees this as a potentially very useful tool for him and his colleagues, that has opened up a world of new client-centred information to which monitoring systems used in the past would never have alerted them.

The MSC method was discussed widely at the conference and generated a great deal of interest. It became clear that Northern agencies and donors wanted to hear a good story, and one that was context specific and peopled with living actors. Inevitably, these stories contain characters, however, not just actors, and it is here that one must be aware of the specific circumstances surrounding the innovative and creative experiences shared at the conference. Certainly in the case of Yedla Padmavathi, it was her individual experience and agency that had launched the innovative process of involving children in M&E. One must ask whether other individuals without her energy, experience or determination could have managed this, or even whether they would have been permitted to do so by the organisation itself.

Chapter 1 by **Tina Wallace** and **Jenny Chapman** implies that, in our current target-bound society, examples of innovative practice like that of Yedla Padmavathi are a rarity. They give a detailed account and analysis of the pressures UK charities find themselves under to establish and implement strict monitoring systems. Much of this revolves around issues of funding and relates to the audit culture that is all pervasive in the UK and which has a knock-on effect through the aid chain. As such, demands for strict reporting in the UK affect partners and Southern NGOs at the grass-roots level. Pressure to perceive and record change in a way that is alien to local culture and ways of working is ultimately disempowering and excluding. This chapter goes on to look at the perverse effects of this type of pressure and shows how it is inimical to development.

Wallace and Chapman's arguments find resonance with some of the comments made by **Brian Pratt** during the conference, on the way in which the UK's bi-lateral aid agency, DFID, is under pressure to behave like other departments in the Government, which in turn are now expected to emulate the business sector. He argued that NGOs do not have the same aims as the private sector and so should not be forced to work in the same way. Similarly, whilst customers in the private sector can make complaints, or change to a different service provider, the 'clients' of development projects are often not able to make their dissatisfaction known, or take their 'business' elsewhere. Already in the UK public sector, doctors and teachers are complaining about the use of target setting, and note its pernicious effects. However, these individuals are in short supply and can potentially form a strong lobby. This is not the case for NGOs in either North or South who are very often in competition for donor funds and are in a weak position when it comes to asserting their own priorities and ways of working.

It would appear that there are certain conditions within organisations and relationships between them that facilitate a more flexible, creative response to the question of M&E. Some of the prerequisites for the right type of thinking are laid out in **James Taylor** and **Sue Soal**'s chapter on measurement (Chapter 5). In a way, this chapter can be seen as a practical response to some of the problems outlined by Dar in Chapter 4, as they call for an end to measurement that is 'anti-developmental' – that is to say, monitoring and reporting processes that do nothing to transform structures within society that restrict human potential. This chapter can be read as the bridge between the two sections of this volume. Although it does not give empirical examples of innovative practice, as the case studies in the same section do, it is written by practitioners, for practitioners and highlights the dangers of the wrong type of measurement as well as suggestions for more useful, developmental measurement.

Peter Morgan, taking the contribution by Taylor and Soal as a starting point, looks in Chapter 2 at the issue of measurement with specific reference to capacity. Although he concludes that assessment of an organisation's capacity is in itself a useful activity, he warns of its potential to be ultimately self-defeating. He notes a paradox in which attempts to measure capacity can in fact reduce the capacity of those being measured, if those involved in the process become fixated upon inappropriate indicators or allow measurement itself to turn into a substitute for capacity development. The second half of Morgan's contribution sets out a series of general principles that could help to improve the measurement of capacity. Echoing other chapters in this volume, he emphasises the need for dialogue and experimentation, and the value that should be placed on subjectivity.

The assumption of *individual responsibility* for monitoring and evaluation processes that assist rather than hinder development is seen by several of the contributors as one of the first steps towards a more useful type of measurement that will challenge some of the power inequalities in the aid sector. The recommendation that all evaluation should begin with oneself was made during the conference and is a useful lesson for all those engaged in development. Nevertheless, discussions during the conference and in this publication, also make a convincing argument that blame for many of the ills of the system lies with 'back' donors. These are perhaps the development actors least likely to evaluate themselves or the impact of abrupt changes they make to policy. But standing up to a donor, whether a US- or European-based INGO or a bi-lateral/multi-lateral agency, in order to push through different ways of working, takes courage and determination and can be risky. It also, at present, seems to be unusual: one participant, summing up her impressions on the final day of the conference, regretted the general lack of passion amongst individuals working in development today, which seems to have come about as a consequence of greater professionalisation of the sector. There are, however, encouraging examples of exactly this type of determination: a paper presented at the conference told of a group of Australian NGOs who, within their umbrella organisation, ACFOA,[3] stood up to AusAid after it published a critical review of the NGO sector that judged them according to inappropriate criteria. As

---

[3] Australian Council for Overseas Aid, now known as ACFID (Australian Council for International Development).

18

a result ACFOA has set out its own definition of the sector against which, in future, their effectiveness should be assessed.

Another example of an NGO behaving 'differently' is that of the UK INGO ActionAid which has changed its reporting and monitoring system in order to allow country programmes to find culturally appropriate and more responsive forms of assessing progress and has done away with some demands for written reports. Even so, as Chapter 8 by **David Chapman** and **Antonella Mancini** shows, this has not been a simple process and there has been resistance at all levels of the organisation. Changing reporting systems has far-reaching consequences as it involves shifts in power relationships. These systems are not contained within an isolated department of an organisation that can be altered overnight; they have significant impact at every level. However, this example of an INGO that has made serious attempts to combat some of the constraints to more flexible monitoring and planning, raises questions about the way in which similar organisations are working. Certainly, ActionAid is not the largest nor the most powerful NGO in the UK. Even so, it is not only attempting to make radical changes to practice within the organisation, it has also refused to give in to pressure from one of its own donors, to adopt a very rigid monitoring and planning framework. ActionAid should stand as an example to others in the sector: it is possible to break through the impasse created by institutional funding regimes. The question remains why other NGOs (within the UK at least) echo the rhetoric of participatory monitoring and evaluation processes, but have not taken the same courageous steps towards its implementation.

Unfortunately, many UK NGOs are currently placing greater weight on global impact monitoring and the ability to compare outcomes from their country programmes across the world. This implies, once more, the use of rigid blueprints for assessment of programmes and a further drift away from flexible approaches that might help place voices from the grass roots at the centre of monitoring and evaluation.

PART ONE

CHAPTER 1

An investigation into the Reality Behind NGO Rhetoric of Downward Accountability

Tina Wallace and Jennifer Chapman

1.1 Introduction

This chapter explores a number of issues arising from the way in which donors and UK non-government organisations (NGOs) structure their reporting and accountability requirements. In doing so the authors challenge some of the fashionable rhetoric on NGO partnerships, participation and bottom-up development. The data is drawn from a wider study of policies and procedures around aid disbursement from the UK to Uganda and South Africa, and the way these shape relationships between donors and Northern and Southern development agencies.[1] The research also analyses how these relationships in turn mould Southern NGO development practice with their partners and beneficiaries; these issues are addressed elsewhere. Here the focus is on broad findings around accountability and impact assessment within aid relationships in UK.

UK NGOs and donors clearly state their commitment to downward accounta-

---

[1] Three teams have been working on these issues since 2000, funded by Nuffield and ESCOR, DFID-UK: Tina Wallace and Jennifer Chapman. South Africa: Lisa Bornstein, Terry Smith, Ansilla Nyar and Isaivani Hyman. Uganda: Martin Kaleeba (ActionAid), staff at CDRN, and Patrick Mulindwa (MISR).

bility and the promotion of local ownership of development in order to achieve sustainable long-term change. However, in practice the growing number of policies and procedures surrounding aid disbursement and accounting ensure that upward accountability and external agendas dominate. This is part of a wider problem of domination by donors of their recipients, which skews relationships and undermines the potential for real partnership.

1.2 The Wider UK Context for Development Aid

The aid sector in the UK does not exist in isolation. It is embedded within wider political and management structures and approaches dominant in the UK. The main characteristic of these is a focus on results, and the ability to demonstrate that they have been achieved. A culture of target-setting and performance management prevails. The new public management focuses on tangible, demonstrable outcomes: organisations and individuals are assessed on their performance, which is often defined by narrow criteria chosen for ease of measurability. Pay and rewards can be related to target achievements encouraging some to tackle easier tasks or even manipulate statistics to achieve targets. These individuals may be better rewarded than those who grapple with complex, intransigent issues that might be closely related to the heart of the problem but which yield few clear and quick results.

The distance between the aspirations encapsulated in defining objectives and target setting and realities on the ground is great. The debates and tensions in the UK around education, health, and police targets are evidence of this. Those trying to implement programmes to achieve targets argue that they are often unrealistic, measure the wrong things (i.e. attendance or drop out rates rather than education quality and relevance), and do not take local reality and diversity into account.

Arguments rage about league tables and targets and how they are often quietly dropped when they are not reached or altered to meet new political agendas. Pressure is sometimes put on management to produce favourable reports. This results/target-driven approach has been critiqued by others, and a small number of examples will suffice to illustrate the dangers inherent in these management approaches and the paradigm of change they represent.

A recent Demos report notes that

> the demands and expectations of central and local government – with their strict performance criteria, emphasis on quantitative outputs and formal participatory structures, such as local strategic partnerships – all act against community projects achieving their aims.

as this report shows, a heavy audit culture often breeds an atmosphere of dis-trust and risk aversion, which encourages uniformity in programme design and inhibits the distinctive contribution that CBOs (Community-Based Organisations) make. (Demos 2003)

The report concludes that the focus should be 'extending and developing people based systems that emphasise ongoing, face-to-face contact between partners and rest on horizontal or mutual forms of accountability, or reducing the number of externally determined indicators and promoting locally determined priorities and outcomes'.

Alisdair MacIntyre, a moral philosopher, argues that it is a modern bureaucrat-ic managerial illusion that people or organisations have the ability to control and shape events. Yet this belief lies at the heart of the new public management. While there is predictability and logic in the world enabling us to plan and engage in long-term projects, 'the pervasive unpredictability in human life also renders all our plans and projects permanently vulnerable and fragile' (MacIntyre 2002:103). He challenges the reliance on concepts of managerial expertise and effectiveness, which create an illusion of social control, but which belie the complexity of the unpredictable and the limits of social control in reality. Yet these limits are denied or ignored and bureaucracies assume greater degrees of power and dominance in an attempt to 'manage' unpredicatability, which a more modest and realistic appraisal of social realities would question. When things go wrong, the belief in the centrality of the tools for achieving targets leads to efforts to invent new and better tools or new ways of measuring change. It can also lead to an insistence on even tighter bureaucratic controls in the mistaken assumption that the 'right' man-agerial approach will control complexity and solve problems.[2] This way of think-ing is clearly often blinkered and self-reinforcing.

In the development world Rondinelli (1993),Schön (1983), Senge (1990) and Shein (1999), among others, have written about the need for open-ended, flexible and responsive approaches to unpredictability and change. Yet these approaches, while often cited, do not appear to shape the way development bureaucracies and agencies undertake development work. Harrison (1995) gives a good description of the impact of tight and output-focused approaches on staff in development organisations, where the pressure to act, achieve and count has overwhelmed efforts to understand, analyse and learn.

A major set of linked concerns was recently presented by Onora O'Neill in the

---

[2] This is evidenced in the development context by the way the World Bank blames national governments for the failure of structural adjustment programmes. Bank policies were not seen as flawed: rather, government failure to follow blueprints correctly was the problem. (See Stiglitz 2002).

Reith lectures. She carefully analysed current attempts in public sector life to control and count:

Central planning may have failed in the former Soviet Union but it is alive and well in Britain today. The new accountability culture aims at ever more perfect administrative control of institutional and professional life (O'Neill 2002: Lecture 3).

She argues that this approach is replacing trust and judgement, 'distorting the proper aims of professional practice and indeed ... damaging professional pride and integrity'. Efforts taken to achieve better performance and results often actually threaten the quality of work, by inhibiting people from using their skills in innovative ways and hedging them in with bureaucratic controls. The pressure for counting and accounting is now so strong that trust, flexibility, ability to adapt to change are undermined.

1.3 The Context for NGOs

This wider political context shapes the thinking and practice of many of the larger and more influential donors to UK NGOs, especially the Department for International Development (DFID) and the European Union (EU). This trend is clearly evident in the Millennium Development Goals (MDGs), which now shape the development agenda in the UK and much of Europe, and the allocation of donor and NGOs' resources – human and financial.[3] While many see the MDGs as ideals, aims to be reached for and a positive mustering of energy on key issues, others see them as concrete targets against which agencies will be measured. Many say the targets will not be met because they are too ambitious and take little account of local realities, or because the political will and resources are lacking for achieving such ambitious aims (UNCTAD 2000). The danger is that these poverty-focused targets dominate current aid spending and yet may be dropped or changed when they appear to be unreachable. Worse, spending may become skewed towards contexts where they can be achieved. For example, reaching some targets in China could dramatically affect the overall MDG percentage achievements; some donors are already saying that they can be met 'excluding Africa'. They risk generating cynicism, demoralisation and inappropriate resource allocation, as target setting has in other UK sectors.

Huddock has convincingly shown the role and power of financial donors in influencing recipient organisations, especially where financial resources are

---

[3] For more information see DFID (1997) and DAC (1999).

scarce. She drew on a wide range of organisational literature, and first hand research in West Africa, to show that survival is a driving force for NGOs, and accessing financial resources is one major key to that survival (Huddock 1996). Other commentators have written about the imperatives of survival and the significance of growth for NGOs (Fowler 1992). As the UK NGO sector expands and overall aid flows fall, so the competition for funding for survival and growth increases (Randell et al. 2002).

1.4 Trends in Donor Funding of UK NGOs

The UK NGO sector is large, complex and diverse, embracing a wide variety of organisations from tiny volunteer-staffed activist NGOs to agencies such as Oxfam, Care and World Vision with worldwide turnovers of hundreds of millions of pounds (Lindenberg and Bryant 2002). Larger organisations, those with shops, and those working through child sponsorship, access varying proportions of their funding from the public (this avenue of funding is not explored here). Overall, compared to the picture in other OECD countries, the UK NGO sector is at the lower end of the scale in the proportion of funds received from government, although this proportion has risen significantly in the last ten years.

Funding experiences are diverse; Oxfam now funds up to fifty per cent of its overseas work through institutional funding; in contrast ActionAid still receives over seventy per cent of funding from direct public giving although it is striving to increase its share of institutional funding[4]. Many medium-sized and smaller NGOs, especially those providing services and specific expertise, raise little untied funding and rely heavily on donor project funding for their continued existence.

Research and existing literature show that very few UK NGOs are entirely independent of institutional and other donors, for many it is a significant or even their only source of funding. These donors include DFID and the EU, foundations and trusts, the two largest independent funding organisations in the UK, Comic Relief and the Community Fund (National Lotteries), and numerous foundations. DFID is by far the largest donor in the UK, although its funding is heavily concentrated in a few large NGOs, with the same five agencies consistently receiving over 45 per cent of total funds annually. The EU is the next largest donor. Many NGOs, even

---

[4] It had initially been thought that agencies with significant amounts of untied funding (from the public for example) would be freer to shape their own systems and procedures. However, it became clear, during the first phase of the research, that they were heavily influenced by the new public management agenda through their trustees, and sometimes their CEOs formerly of the business sector. They were also influenced by their close relations with key donors.

those with significant independent funding sources, are putting considerable effort into raising more funding from these sources, and want to increase their share of this income by winning large contracts as well as accessing earmarked NGO funding lines. Recently, NGOs without access to public donations have been very vulnerable to shifts in donor agendas, funding delays, and changing priorities.

Previous research has highlighted the critical role of donors in shaping how UK NGOs work and what they do, while boards of trustees and chief executives also play a significant role (Wallace et al. 1997). The data from the research project on which this chapter is based strongly suggests the wider donor context has changed significantly and that donor influence has increased further over the past four years.

The complexities of the NGO sector and the changing priorities of different funding regimes available to UK NGOs mean that these changes impact differently on NGOs according to their size, origins, and focus (Wallace and Chapman 2002). One of the most significant funding shifts that has affected the sector has been DFID's move away from funding NGOs as key conduits of aid for service delivery, and a return to greater reliance on government. Funding to governments has greatly increased through both budget support and sector-wide funding, especially in sub-Saharan Africa. Poverty Reduction Strategy Papers (PRSPs) now govern aid disbursement to many countries worldwide, and NGO roles are expected to shift from direct provision of services and support for the poor, to building local civil society and ensuring the accountability of governments for their use of funds. They are also expected to provide some services within the broad government plan framework, and to access funding for this directly from government and not from donors.

DFID's Joint Funding Scheme, which supported a wide range of sector-focused and specialist NGOs over many years, has been closed and the new Civil Society Department has replaced it. This has introduced a new set of funding mechanisms. Large (and more recently a few specialist) NGOs were invited to apply for partnership funding, administered under programme partnership agreements (PPAs). These PPAs replaced the old system of block grants that were previously available only to five major NGOs (Oxfam, Christian Aid, CAFOD, Save the Children Fund and VSO) and included more agencies. The Civil Society Challenge Fund (CSCF) is a fund for non-PPA agencies, but providing much lower levels of funding than the Joint Funding Scheme. New criteria govern access and the stress is on work on advocacy and rights, promoting local civil society and ensuring government accountability. Funding is not available to agencies doing basic service delivery only, although decisions about what constitutes service delivery and civil society building, and the appropriate ways to promote rights in contexts of weak, corrupt or non-existent states, often appear arbitrary.

Two newer and expanding sources of funding from DFID for UK NGOs are contracts and direct funding in-country. DFID increasingly puts out to tender contracts for work considered critical to their overall strategy in a country, and NGOs are invited to bid for these alongside private consultants, companies and governments. Only large NGOs with sufficient resources are in a position to compete for these contracts, which are often worth millions of pounds over three to five years. Direct in-country funding is administered from DFID's country offices in line with their country strategies; different funding strategies are developing in individual country offices. Increasingly many UK NGOs are positioning themselves locally to be eligible to access this funding.

The net result of these changes is that DFID funding for medium and small UK NGOs has dropped dramatically over the last two years.

The EU experienced a crisis around the administration of the NGO co-financing budget line and ceased all new grants in 2000, cutting off access to vital funding for many UK NGOs. It has since resumed its programme and now NGOs must present their proposals within the framework of the calls for proposals organised by the Commission on an annual basis. This new system is intended to introduce greater transparency and management effectiveness as well as allow the European Community (EC) to define political priorities and set targets. It has led to an increase in the number of NGOs applying for funds. However, many NGOs which in the past received regular EU funding through the NGO budget line, no longer find it possible to access funding due to increased competition, the complexity of the bids, new contract conditions[5], lack of staff time and capacity, and the fact that their work no longer falls within the designated themes. The new funding regime appears to favour large, complex agencies able to meet the bidding and contract requirements and with the staff capacity to respond quickly to new themes. It thereby undermines the stated aim of the budget line to increase the EC's capacity to support risk.

The volume of lottery funding, now known as the Community Fund, has fallen in recent years due to the decline in popularity of the lottery. The international programme has come under scrutiny and has been unable to maintain continuity: there was recently a total hiatus in funding for 18 months. Funding resumed in 2003, with new criteria, guidelines and application cycles. The sum to be disbursed is around £11 million, compared with highs of £17 million three years ago. Comic Relief funding, in contrast, has risen and is becoming one of the few real alternative sources of funding for many small and medium-sized NGOs. They disbursed almost £20 million to NGOs working in Africa over the two years 1999 and 2000.

---

[5] In January 2002 a standard contract was introduced that imposes new conditions drawn up with the private sector in mind. For example, for any project of 1 million euros or above the implementing organisation needs bank guarantees that they could pay the money back if they did not meet the terms of the contract.

The money available from foundations and small donor trust funds, which are often more flexible and responsive to NGO requests and more prepared to take risks, has been declining because of the fall in stock market values. Some have revised their strategic focus and changed their funding to four or five large grants rather than peppering a lot of agencies with smaller grants (e.g. Barings and Nuffield). This again has impacted on many small and medium NGOs. In addition many NGOs have seen the value of their reserves decrease dramatically as the stock market has declined.

1.5 Donor Policies and Procedures

Along with the decline in money for NGOs, particularly funding for their own, rather than donor-led agendas, there has been a rise in the number and complexity of donor demands on UK NGOs. DFID now require logframes for all CSCF funding, in spite of some senior staff claiming that logframes would disappear by the end of the 1990s because of known flaws and difficulties.[6] Agencies are being encouraged to formulate their global strategies into logframes for their PPA agreements now, and DFID reviews of UK NGOs are undertaken against logframes at the project, programme, country and global levels. Formal contracts are very tightly regulated and defined. Strategic plans, policies around gender, advocacy and conflict, for example, detailed reporting requirements, tight and difficult-to-change budgets, and retrospective funding have all become part of DFID funding. The EU has always been a controlling, bureaucratic and relatively inflexible funder; their recent problems with accountability and transparency mean that this will certainly continue.

Over the years the Community Fund has increased its demands and tightened its focus on strategic themes; the application form has expanded to almost fifty pages in response to both NGO concerns and changes in donor agendas. They require NGOs to show wide coverage, impact and effectiveness, and the ability to link service delivery and policy work; also to show that their work gives good value for money and takes into consideration current development issues. Comic Relief has essentially kept its core priority themes and focus over several years now and has largely adhered to its original principles for grant giving.

The Community Fund, and increasingly Comic Relief, rely on external assessors[7]

---

[6] This was one of the formal responses to phase one of the research, where the researchers were told they had focused overly on logframes as it was a tool on the wane.

[7] The Community Fund uses temporary assessors in large numbers while Comic Relief now has a relatively small number of long-term assessors working with their grants officers.

so there is a tendency to focus more on quantitative issues that can be checked, such as evidence of clear policies, procedures and systems – for which Community Fund has a complex system of numerical scoring – rather than difficult qualitative issues. These issues include assessment of and support for risk taking; understanding the strengths and weaknesses of relations with Southern partners and how to improve these relationships; how to enable organisational strengthening and improve development work; and how to ensure the work is responsive to local people in the context of written project plans. Comic Relief grapples with these complex, hard to measure issues. However, external donor trends and UK management thinking inevitably impact on staff and assessors and tend to push them to adopt more dominant approaches.

A central concern for most institutional donors is to cut transaction costs, resulting in contracting out and a bias towards working with fewer, large NGOs. In some countries DFID is contracting an organisation to run their direct funding for NGOs, elsewhere an NGO is selected as lead agency in a bid and manages the programme for DFID. The commitment to competition means that NGOs must compete with each other and with government and the private sector for donor contracts. Often this was money that was automatically channelled through the NGO sector before, yet there appears to be little analysis of the costs of time and energy incurred in this approach nor is it clear how criteria for effectiveness are judged.[8]

The key donors do not meet regularly to share their ideas systematically[9], or to discuss new polices or procedures and the implications of these for the NGO sector. There is no clear donor position or conceptualisation about the role for the UK NGO sector in development. Donor staff interviewed were not sure whether it mattered that some, usually larger, NGOs were growing and benefiting from new donor agendas, while others, usually smaller, were being squeezed and even disappearing. There was no evidence of analysis about the value and roles of different types of NGOs, and which performed best in different contexts. Changes were

---

[8] The problems of assessing aid effectiveness are known to all NGOs grappling with impact assessment frameworks, and also to DFID as evidenced in their recent draft Development Effectiveness Review 2002. This highlighted many weaknesses in definitions, available information and methodologies which prevent DFID having a good assessment of what makes effective development. In spite of DFID's inability really to understand the impact of its spending on development or poverty alleviation, it continues to demand that NGOs demonstrate their impact, although they are far smaller players than DFID and often working in the most challenging areas of poverty and development.

[9] INTRAC has facilitated two international donor workshops in the UK, Development Initiatives hosted a global workshop of donors for DFID in 2000, and this research project has facilitated two small donor workshops. Bi-lateral meetings take place and there are continuing attempts to meet more regularly on the part of some UK donors.

not apparently being driven by evaluation or analysis of the performance of NGOs (i.e. by hard evidence), but by internal ideology and agendas.

The impact of the tightening donor context may perhaps in some instances be intended and in others unexpected. Some staff at DFID clearly thought there were too many NGOs in the UK and shifts that squeeze out are seen as positive, almost regardless of which NGOs disappear; others appeared oblivious to the shifts taking place in the sector as a result of donor changes. Currently, these issues are not properly analysed or planned; no donor agency interviewed had even asked the question about the impact that changes in funding is having on the shape of the UK NGO sector, let alone how this will impact on development work with their partners. New management systems are adopted, new conditionalities added for a whole variety of organisational and ideological reasons with little thought for how these changes will in turn shape development thinking and practice.

1.6 Some Key Consequences

In aggregate, funding changes favour the more powerful and well established NGOs in the UK, which are growing rapidly and investing major resources in raising institutional donor funding[10], and those able to adapt to and deliver on the latest focus on a rights-based approach and advocacy work. The current belief that a narrowly defined form of 'policy-focused advocacy' is an essential or even the key aspect of all development work risks a bias against those working with the poor directly.

A number of small and medium sized NGOs no longer fit the currently desired profile and find themselves in financial difficulties; some have relocated (e.g. ACORD and SOS Sahel), some have merged (e.g. within the HIV/AIDS sector), others are discussing merger or even closure. Many are undertaking careful risk assessments to ensure they are solvent and financial security – or the lack of it – dominates many trustee discussions.[11] One group of 11 medium sized NGOs (with incomes of £1–10 million) have formed a consortium, DOMINGO, to explore how to weather these financial storms and growing donor conditionalities. Many are now operating close to their financial limits and much time is spent analysing the new policy agendas, whether they are doing unique and valuable work or could close without detriment to development work (though obviously with high costs to their staff and partners).

---

[10] One agency has over 30 fundraisers working to raise funds solely from government and multi-lateral donors.

[11] Personal communication with a range of UK NGO staff and trustees.

As funding becomes tighter, competition increases. Competition exacerbates some of the existing deficiencies and problems in the NGO sector in the UK, and increasingly allows donors to set the agenda. One of the most alarming consequences is the evident fear and secrecy within the entire 'aid chain'. These are strong words, but words that accurately describe many current relationships. The hallmark of doing research with NGOs is that they almost always request confidentiality; they do not wish to incur the displeasure of, or damage their image with, either donors or the wider public by sharing issues of concern openly. This situation has worsened since phase 1 of the research with very few UK organisations or individuals wanting to be identified directly with some of the critical issues emerging from the research[12]. This is also true for NGOs in Africa receiving funds from UK NGOs; at every level people will only open up freely if they are guaranteed anonymity.

This lack of openness and trust between the funded and the funders occurs at each level. While there are exceptions where trust and confidence between individuals and organisations allow for open discussion and dialogue, the hallmark at present is secrecy and a fear of being seen to rock the boat.

As the donors are so dominant, UK NGOs are under pressure to meet the donors' demands and perceived needs rather than those of other stakeholders. It also leads to the mushrooming of claims by NGOs about what they can achieve with relatively small amounts of money, called 'promise inflation'. As they strive to meet the ever growing demands of donors, they claim they are able to:

- do hands-on work and advocacy,
- link the micro to the macro,
- network and build networks elsewhere,
- build local organisations to hold governments to account for their use of funding,
- promote partnerships,
- undertake policy work,
- innovate,
- work with the private and public sectors,
- take a rights-based approach,
- do poverty-focused work effectively,
- demonstrate their impact,
- be cost effective and have a wide reach and influence.

---

[12] Two notable exceptions in this round of the research are ActionAid in the UK and in Uganda, and Womankind. Both are striving to become open and transparent organisations, in line with stated values.

There is an upward spiral of claims in order to secure funding. Reporting then becomes a process of proving these myriad claims were met.

Another result of donor domination is the adoption of donor tools, often uncritically. While an assessment of the impact of many of these tools has never been undertaken (this research attempts to be the start of an analysis of how these tools shape development thinking) they have been freely embraced. Indeed they are often at the heart of the training and capacity building programmes undertaken by UK NGOs with their partners in the South. The same is true for donor reporting demands that are passed on to the next level, along with ever tightening budget requirements.

These factors all combine to make NGOs defensive and secretive, as they are trying and claiming to achieve far more than is possible, and they have become often uncritical of their own and donor practice. Their critiques of donor conditionalities remain largely unvoiced[13] and these conditionalities are actively passed down to their partner organisations. Increasingly NGOs and CBOs requesting funding in South Africa and Uganda are expected to conform to a similar set of structures, systems, policies and procedures, forcing them to resemble their donor NGOs and each other. This is squeezing out the diversity and range of alternative perspectives and approaches in civil societies in different cultures and contexts. Questions raised by Southern partners about these pressures to conform to externally set criteria are usually not passed on to donors.

Evaluations or learning that raise real questions about this way of working and NGOs' ability to meet all their claims, or which highlight real weaknesses in organisational processes or development work are not shared. While the World Bank places highly critical evaluations and reviews on its website, NGOs feel they cannot afford to be so open; their continued existence or growth[14] depends on keeping up the cycle of rising claims and providing evidence that they are meeting them. The growing reporting requirements increase this pressure to show in a positive light everything that has been done. However, at the same time this increases cynicism, among staff, donors and partners, about development and their effectiveness – and this in turn leads to increasing pressure to tell good stories to counter that cynicism.

---

[13] There are some notable exceptions where some agencies come together to input into donor debates or to question donor procedures (e.g. around the DFID initiated debate on civil society in 1998). But the voices are infrequent and muted even around issues such as the Development Effectiveness Review of DFID's work, or the lack of support they felt from the Secretary of State for development when Clare Short held that post.

[14] For small and medium sized NGOs the issue is one of existence. For larger NGOs with independent incomes the issue is probably far more one of growth and a desire to receive contract funding, and to be part of policy discussions at the highest levels with donors.

These demands weigh heavily and can take more time and energy than is spent listening to and responding to the needs of the people with whom the NGOs work. They face dilemmas hard to resolve when the needs and perspectives of those they want to support clash with those of their donors; different NGOs experience and handle these tensions and contradictions at different levels. This becomes a skewed process, where upward accountability risks distorting organisations and diverting staff away from working responsively with local people; this in turn risks the commitment to sustainability through real participation, local ownership and changes to inequalities that keep so many poor.[15]

The research does not deny the agency of individuals and NGOs within this broad context, and there are some startling exceptions to the broad trends. Yet the findings show that the dominant pressures come from meeting the demands of donors in order to survive or grow, rather than for finding ways to prioritise the needs of local people, beneficiaries or local organisations. Many donor imperatives such as targets, demonstrating effectiveness, measurable indicators, are also imperatives for board members and chief executives, who come from the wider business culture in the UK described earlier. Once the larger NGOs take up policies and procedures, the pressure on small and medium sized NGOs increases further, making it even harder for them to buck the trends and behave differently.

1.7 Issues of Monitoring and Evaluation

UK NGOs and donors are working in a wider context that reinforces the culture of bureaucratic control, measurement of concepts and change, proving effectiveness to auditors, managers and potential critics. These are reinforcing the power of those with the money and ensure an upward focus within NGOs. They undermine concepts of partnership which require two way negotiation, listening, and downward accountability. Yet much of the rhetoric and commitment around development work focuses on learning and the learning organisation, listening to the voices on the ground, working bottom-up and participatively, in a process and not a blueprint way. The arguments for taking a learning approach are well understood: the issues of development are complex, the problems challenging and difficult to address, the constraints of poor contexts often militate against even achieving the activities planned. There are many manuals and policies within NGOs around participatory monitoring and evaluation, becoming a learning organisation, and bottom-up planning.

---

[15] These dynamics were clear in the interviews and observational work with NGOs in South Africa and Uganda.

Exploring donor conditionalities and the response of UK NGOs suggests that while there is a real commitment to these values and approaches, in practice the drive to show control of events, to muster evidence to support an input-output rational logical model of change, which is predictable and manageable, dominates. The next section focus on the procedures and demands around monitoring and evaluation in the UK, to explore how far the arguments presented so far are upheld or questioned by realities around accountability in the aid chain.

Monitoring and Evaluation of the New PPAs

By the end of 2001, 11 UK NGOs had signed PPAs with DFID, gaining programme funding for three years. To win a PPA, an NGO is expected to show how its work contributes to DFID's own targets, that it is financially secure and well managed and that it can report effectively against the joint strategic objectives agreed in the PPA.

These PPAs have a number of advantages for the recipient NGOs. The funding is not tied to specific projects, allowing flexibility in how it is used. Many NGOs say that not having to account project by project cuts down on paperwork and allows time for more strategic reflection.

The PPA seems to relieve us of a lot of bureaucratic reporting. In theory it allows us to insert our own agenda on M&E and learning. In the past we have done evaluations we wouldn't otherwise have done for DFID. The question is does it give DFID greater leverage over our strategic plan? I don't think it does. (Interview with NGO PPA Recipient Staff)

In most cases (VSO being the exception) the PPA agreement only provides a small percentage of the NGO's total funding. But they have a symbolic importance beyond the size of the funding:

DFID PPA funding is only a small percentage of our total funding, but politically it is big. It gives leverage elsewhere. (Interview with NGO PPA Recipient Staff)

However, a close look at these new funding tools also reveals a number of tensions. Some of these are particularly pertinent to the question of upward and downward accountability.

Firstly by their very nature the PPAs are intended only for NGOs that are contributing directly to DFID's own priorities and targets. The NGO must show how their global strategic goals are compatible with DFID's own. This supports a trend already seen in many larger UK NGOs, of planning strategically at the global level. While some NGOs have based this on consultation with staff around the world, others have done this work centrally, and few have consulted with partners on their strategies. Strategies developed collaboratively often change in the final drafts, when UK-based staff adjust the plans to meet new global agendas set by the World Bank, think tanks, donors and other agencies. The process of strategic planning can, and does, lead to tensions between the global agendas and local realities; staff on the ground often struggle to see the fit between the vision and over-arching strategies and their day to day work. DFID will only fund parts of the strategy, those that comply most closely with their own.

Within the PPA there is an emphasis on reporting on aggregate impact at the global level. Yet reporting at an aggregate level on work that is happening in different ways in different countries remains very challenging, and can easily become distorting and misleading. DFID's inability to undertake this kind of analysis and impact assessment itself is clear from the draft Development Effectiveness Report they commissioned to explore DFID's impact on poverty reduction in 2002. Earlier attempts to assess the impact of ODA (Overseas Development Assistance: now DFID) on poverty, prior to 1997, took a more complex set of analytical tools and criteria for analysing what changes ODA had been involved in promoting in four countries in the previous ten years. That study, headed by Andrew Shepherd, which tried to address many of the complex issues of definitions, measurement, what criteria and scales to employ and what data to use to measure changes, was never published. Some of the findings were, however, used in subsequent DFID country strategy papers.

Each of the five NGOs that make up the British Overseas Agencies Group (BOAG) agencies are busy developing their own systems for gathering and aggregating data to report against global strategic objectives. These are complex and do pay more attention to upward rather than downward accountability, though they are all concerned to ensure partners are properly included. The clear purpose is to meet DFID and trustee demands for evidence of effectiveness, not partner needs for learning and accountability from the UK NGO. Where the original impetus came from for these organisation wide systems is open to debate. Some agencies claim that they were planning to do this anyway and that the PPA negotiations gave them added motivation, others are quite clear that the original impetus came from fear of imminent evaluations by DFID. Others saw expressed tensions between the desire of the international directors for information at the global level and other initiatives within the organisation designed to improve downward accountability.[16]

The contradictions between collecting information to prove effectiveness for further funding, for developing upward and downward accountability, and for critical learning remain unresolved in all of the existing systems. The global systems

---

[16] These evolving systems were presented at a BOAG evaluation group meeting hosted by ActionAid in January 2003.

are intended to prove global impact, and yet most of these large NGOs now work through partners. How they can aggregate and thus claim the work of others is not resolved. The question of the effect this has on partners is barely debated.

All the systems require considerable time and resources to set up initially and to implement. In most cases there was not prior recognition of the full implications of this in terms of the staff time and support required. All the systems make efforts to include partners in reflections in different ways, but in no cases were partners significantly involved in designing or drawing up the systems. The questions of who defines change, and whether it is positive or negative, have not been adequately addressed.

There is a lot of rhetoric about learning as a main driver for the global impact reporting. Some agencies are specifically encouraging the reporting and discussion of problems and difficulties in projects. Yet there is little to no discussion about how meaningful learning can take place from interventions that are unique and messy in very different contexts. There is also little analysis about how funding and power relationships might make it difficult for honest discussion around failure and problems.[17] There is general scepticism about whether the relationship with DFID can be a meaningful partnership allowing for mutual learning:

> I see the PPA as a contract for collaboration, not a real partnership. I am not hopeful there will be real learning or support. One problem is that there is a huge turnover of staff at DFID. The text of the PPA was agreed with one person, the Memorandum of Understanding and financial matters with another. Some are in London and some Scotland. (Interview with NGO PPA Recipient Staff)

Some NGOs are making genuine attempts to improve downwards or sideways accountability. For example ActionAid and Save the Children Fund provide forums for their other stakeholders to criticise and feedback on their work, and ActionAid is trying to improve financial transparency at the country and local levels. But overall the pressures outlined above push systems overwhelmingly towards upward accountability.

Despite the wide criticism of logframes for anything but the most straightforward event management, and their obvious unsuitability for more complex programmes, many feel logframes can be scaled up to cover global approaches. With the PPAs the thrust from DFID has been towards reporting against a logframe. While this was strongly and successfully resisted in some agencies during the initial PPA negotiations, there has been recent renewed pressure to conform. A new

---

[17] In the BOAG evaluation group meeting mentioned above, Save the Children Fund and ActionAid were the only two organisations that addressed this issue.

agency, the PARC, has been set up to help UK NGOs to meet DFID's monitoring, evaluation and reporting requirements, and some advisors have taken a strong logframe, quantitative bias. Those NGOs who were trying to balance learning approaches and measuring impact have to struggle against the reintroduction of uniform systems and requirements.[18]

This begs the question about why strong, large and relatively powerful NGOs, who do not receive a high percentage of their funding through the PPAs, conform to these demands. The answer may lie in several areas. First, these demands fit with those from trustees and chief executives who want data on impact for profile and accountability purposes. Second, as organisations grow, their focus and rationale shifts, and many of the large NGOs now place a high value on strong relations with DFID for influencing policy and are becoming (or wish to become) part of government delegations and discussion groups. Third, while the PPA funds are small, other funds from DFID are potentially vast for these NGOs; maintaining cordial relations is a critical strategy for their aim to be included in large contracts and global debates.

Finally there are rising demands within the development sector to understand what difference they are making. Yet NGOs are intervening in highly complex social and political structures, which they have no control over, and are trying to address major problems with a mix of local and global roots. Also their role is often not to promote the changes themselves, but to support and encourage local actors and processes. Identifying significant change in the short term, in such contexts, while desirable, is unattainable and results in a distortion of development resources and work (Kaplan 2001).

Monitoring and Evaluation around EU and DFID (and other Bi-lateral) Contracts

Reporting against contracts is difficult for many NGOs. The requirements are rigorous and detailed, but it is often hard to ensure that the staff implementing the project really understand what data are needed for accountability. The financial reporting is especially demanding; 'onerous' is how it is often described. Many NGO internal systems for reporting and accountability are not set up to meet criteria set out in contracts, and staff in fundraising departments often have to do additional work to ensure that the reports meet donor high standards.

The logframes required for bidding for EU and DFID contracts, the detailed budgets with clear justifications of all budget line items and the need to explain clearly and logically the links between the concept and explicit activities make

---

[18] For a critique of attempts to combine evaluations for very different purposes see for example the writings of Allan Kaplan in the Annual Reports of CDRA, South Africa. www.cdra.org.za

preparing bids, implementation and accounting very demanding for NGOs. Specialised staff are often needed, or consultants are brought in to support these processes. One large NGO said that UK NGOs are ill equipped to compete with private companies for many of these contracts, even though they are often better placed to do good work on the ground. Taking on contracts inevitably ties NGOs tightly to donor agendas and reporting requirements, which has implications for both implementation and where they focus their accountability mechanisms.

Monitoring and Evaluation (and Reporting) on Projects

It is often noted that projects are an inappropriate vehicle for change and development yet in reality much funding continues to be disbursed through them, and reporting against projects remains almost universal. NGOs with projects funded through the Civil Society Challenge Fund, Comic Relief and the Community Fund have to report against their project frameworks.

For CSCF these projects have to be presented in logframes, and reporting is tied closely to the inputs, outputs, outcomes and impact delineated in the logframe. Indicators are requested at the time of the project proposal and subsequently monitored. While the Community Fund does not require a logframe, they report that increasingly NGOs in the UK find this format one they feel comfortable with and against which they have learned to report.

Comic Relief has clear, but more fluid, reporting guidelines that NGOs need to follow. They have had cause for concern about late and poor reporting, but increasingly monitor the receipt of reports and require them before the disbursement of the next tranche of funding. NGOs report against their project proposals and many report a lessening of flexibility around changes and new directions, compared with their past experiences of Comic Relief.

All funders interviewed as part of the research raised issues around NGO reporting, including the poor quality of some reports, late reporting, and lack of clarity of the authorship of the report. They have worked to improve the timing and quality of NGO reporting on their projects in recent years, though they have not found a way to ensure that the reports they receive are 'the voice' of the field staff or beneficiaries. Many donors are asking for additional information to get at this – significant change stories, focus group discussions, case studies and more qualitative ways of reporting, although these usually remain an addition to the other forms of reporting. NGOs often feel caught by these demands; on the one hand donors want reporting against tight criteria laid out in the funding proposal, on the other they want 'the voice from the field'. People at field level may be monitoring different changes and responding to different needs on the ground and their reports may have to be reworked later to meet donor standards.

Field staff and partners often find themselves involved in two sets of evaluation and reporting processes, one for the organisation's effectiveness audit, and the

other for local learning. ActionAid recognised this and excused all country programme staff from the annual reporting processes and encouraged local participatory reflection and learning. However, this left the agency with inadequate compa-
rable data for global annual reporting and there is growing pressure on staff to try
and do both in future. Their experience highlighted very clearly the tensions and
contradictions between local level processes and accountability and organisational
needs for reporting to trustees and donors.

While many agencies say they encourage partners to write their own reports
and present their own voice, the research findings show that in most agencies these
reports are revised to meet donor requirements as they rise through the aid chain.
NGOs in the UK have to ensure that reporting meets donor requirements and often
cannot allow partners and local groups to keep their own voice when they explain
the work and achievements in terms that may not easily translate into UK contexts.
The raw realities of field level experience often disappear within these reporting
structures, and there is an understandable tendency to focus on success. Although
donors say they encourage reporting on failure and learning from experience, UK
NGOs cite too many examples where they feel their funding has been threatened
because of discussing problems openly. The current systems are rigid, built not on
trust but on paperwork, which inhibits the real sharing of the challenges of development in practice.

Two further areas are nearly always glossed over in reports to donors. One is
the issue of relationships; the quality of donor–UK NGO relations, UK NGO–partner relations and partner NGO/CBO relations with beneficiaries are rarely discussed. These relationship issues do not feature in the logframe so reporting on
them is not required by most reporting systems. A second area is that of methodology or development practice. The ways in which NGOs are trying to work to
empower women, or enable networks to develop, or to address poverty of the most
excluded are again not part of the logframe analysis and so are not usually
analysed or reflected upon in the reporting process.

The research identified a number of specific issues around the use of logframes
for reporting that ensure that the pressure remains for upward accountability, rather
than accountability to beneficiaries. These issues are additional to the concerns
raised by other commentators about the use of logframes as the central development management tool.[19]

Reporting against the logframe excludes so many issues critical to development
practice including the nature of the relationships built around development
processes; the real constraints of implementation and limits of the control of the

[19] See papers presented by Das Gupta, Margaret Kakande and Ros Eyben at a workshop
on Power and Partnerships, hosted by the Institute of Development Studies, Sussex
University, in May 2002. www.ids.ac.uk

project; and local understandings of the problems and ways of addressing them. While modifications to logframes have been developed, to make them more participatory and responsive, they remain a tool based on linear logic, on beliefs about ways of managing and controlling change not drawn from local understanding or experience. Partners report consistently that logframes do not support their work in practice: they are irrelevant or distorting and so are often set aside. Yet when it comes to reporting they have to be taken up again. The real challenges and dilemmas of the development process on the ground are then put aside as they struggle to report against the paper documentation.

The universal nature of the logframe implicitly devalues different ways of approaching planning and implementation in different countries and different cultural perceptions of how to promote development. It cuts partners and NGO staff out of local systems of discussion and accountability by placing a very high value on an externally designed and driven tool. Partners' own ideas and processes for monitoring and reporting are subsumed by logframes. The concepts in Logical Framework Approach (LFA) are often hard to grasp and hard to use, so a great deal of time is spent teaching this tool to staff and partners. This engenders a respect for the tool because it is seen as professional and technical. LFA is certainly becoming the dominant mode of reporting and analysis, even though staff know it does not provide a good guide for work on the ground. This disconnect between the planning and reporting tool, and what happens in reality, is deeply damaging for the reporting process, which is inevitably cut off from implementation experiences.

The logframe is experienced by many as a tool of control and accountability. Along with financial reporting and accounting systems it is a system of controlling activities and inputs. It attempts to replace the need for trust, local knowledge and understanding, and good working relations with partners, with a universal system. People in the UK understand LFA better and can more easily manipulate data to fit its reporting requirements; inevitably they revise and correct reports coming from the field to ensure they fulfil LFA reporting systems. This distorts the process system of accountability and learning.

The pressures of the LFA and the concepts of managing change that it carries within it means that upward accountability in line with certain formats dominates. There are no similar systems or pressures pushing NGOs to adopt processes of downward accountability. Some UK NGOs do support local participatory processes but they tend to be isolated examples of other ways of reporting and recording progress. They include participatory reflection with communities, partner forums, joint working on significant change stories, and using PRA as a monitoring and evaluation tool with local people. They are presented further elsewhere in this volume; they are, however, usually an addition to the dominant modes of reporting, not a replacement.

1.8 Reporting: Some Further Reflections

The pressures around reporting are so keenly felt within many UK NGOs that it is worth spending a little more time on this issue. Most NGOs interviewed as part of the research said that reporting requirements were too complex and that far too much time was spent on it. The demands and time taken to meet them are constantly rising. Mawdsley et al. (2002) and Brehm (2001) endorse this finding. The demands from donors around more systematic and regular reporting – some projects have to report quarterly and others every six months, or annually – have a knock-on effect. Some UK NGOs demand monthly reporting, financial and narrative, from their project officers. Often these require reporting on achievements and impact after a very short time. Reports usually have to relate closely to the aims and objectives set out in the logframe and even when changes have been carefully explained they are not always accepted. When evaluations are carried out for example by DFID, often the evaluator will be given the original logframe and this will be the yardstick against which the project is assessed, regardless of subsequent changes.

Donors have the power to sanction poor reporting, weak project management, and other failures by refusing further funding. The partners and communities have no sanctions to impose on NGOs. Yet it is often not easy for NGOs and communities to find ways to fit their diverse, complex realities and actual experiences into tight reporting formats. Many find it hard to write well in English, and this may require their NGO partner to edit, change and improve their reports for donors, or even to write them, often leading to a glossing over of difficulties and complexities in the process. At each level there is often editorial control before the report reaches the donor. There is no parallel structure to enable downward accountability, or even information sharing. Often local partners and beneficiaries are completely unaware of the key project documents, the aims and objectives of the project as presented to donors, and the nature of the organisation they are involved with. They may have a very poor grasp of the overall purpose of the NGO that funds the project they are engaged in, nor understand why they came or why they leave.

The research found that often local staff of UK or international NGOs working in a country field office have a very weak understanding of the overall strategic plan of the agency they are employed by, and a limited grasp of their global activities. They feel far from the centre and have little power or influence over the work of the wider organisation. They may be writing or editing reports from partners to go back to donors they have a limited understanding of, and many said they did not know if their projects were funded by DFID, Community Fund, Comic Relief or another international agency. They tend to work within standard procedures, developed by each INGO for use across all their projects and designed to meet the needs of financial accounting and accountability at headquarters and donors. It was startling to see that not one agency with a PPA agreement with DFID had passed this flexible funding mechanism on to their partners, something DFID staff were completely unaware of and shocked to hear about. The flexibilities UK NGOs do enjoy *vis-à-vis* PPAs, funding by Comic Relief for example, or foundations, are rarely passed on to their field staff or partners.

Finally, a common complaint was that after all the effort and time put into reporting they rarely receive any feedback. Reports seem to disappear into a vacuum. Questions or comments, if they come, may arrive up to a year later, sometimes taking even longer. The learning and interaction potential around reporting appears to be largely missing, and many staff in NGO headquarters and in overworked donor offices admitted to having little time to really read and absorb the volume of reports that cross their desks. DFID contracts out the work of managing the project cycle, resulting in different people giving often conflicting feedback to NGOs on their work and reports. Others leave reports unread for months. This causes despondency and even cynicism in those that write them. Those that receive them often feel overwhelmed by the paperwork, and the imperative to get on with the next phase prevents time for reflection and feedback.

1.9 Conclusions

Current policies and procedures around the project cycle and the disbursement of aid from donors to UK NGOs, and from UK NGOs to Southern NGOs are dominated by tools developed in the UK, Europe or US based on new public management thinking and approaches. These tools put more emphasis and importance on the needs of the donors and on paperwork than on the realities of development processes and accounting to the people who are the supposed beneficiaries of the whole process: the poor in communities across Africa, Asia and Latin America.

In Africa these procedures shape the discussions and debates between donors and 'partners', pushing partner agendas into the shade and encouraging them to learn the procedures required by the donors. The focus on written systems as opposed to face to face or other forms of communication reflects the needs of Northern organisations, but ignores dominant forms of communication in the South. This approach to the disbursement and accounting can be read as an extension of the historical dominance of the North where Southern organisations continue to be disempowered. It has a real impact on the possibility of building real partnerships and potentially engenders negative relationships, something that is well analysed in a new UNDP publication by African writers called *Winning the war against humiliation* (Tevoedjre 2002).

The data emerging from this three-country case study suggests that if the rhetoric on local ownership, building strong local civil societies, bottom-up development, and local sustainability are to have real meaning, these policies and procedures need revisiting. They carry within them issues and values that need re-examining and changing. In the UK many practitioners in their fields contest results-based approaches, target setting, quantitative reporting, and onerous systems of measurement. The problems they recognise become far more acute when these systems are exported. They do not translate well, nor do they serve the needs of people for whom the world is a complex, contingent place and where the issues they are grappling with are often huge and multi-faceted. The challenges of working to combat poverty in places where conflict, HIV/AIDS, aid dependent economies, poor public services and debt are daily realities, cannot be logically boxed and rationally controlled, nor easily measured and accounted for. Many of the processes that NGOs and people themselves are involved in may take generations to yield sustainable social and economic change. The current obsession with almost instant, demonstrable impact is distorting and needs challenging at every level.

CHAPTER 2

Measuring the Development of Capacity: Is it Still a Good Idea?

Peter Morgan

2.1 Introduction

Since the early 1990s, the international development community has been championing two ideas: capacity development and results-based management.[1] Both have gone from being sporadic interventions to becoming accepted orthodoxy.[2] And both are relatively simple ideas in theory if not in practice. Capacity is about the ability, mainly of organisations and groups of organisations, to perform or to deliver some sort of developmental value to stakeholders, clients and citizens. *Measurement* concerns the systematic assessment of this strengthened capacity using indicators. In principle, the marriage of these two approaches – the measurement of capacity and/or capacity development – sounds like a good idea.

But is it? Beneath the orthodoxy, a more complex picture emerges as the marriage gets beyond the honeymoon stage. Reading other chapters in this book such as those by Wallace and Chapman (Chapter 1) and Taylor and Soal (Chapter 5)

---

[1] I use the term 'capacity development' in this article and equate it with the newer generation of terms such as 'capacity enhancement'.

[2] A recent study in CIDA found that the proportion of projects within the overall CIDA portfolio that listed capacity development as a key or prime objective rose dramatically in the 1990s from 9.6 per cent of projects in 1990/91 to almost 74 per cent in 2002/01. See Lavergne et al. (2004) p. i.

gives rise to a pervasive sense of unease about some current practices. Once implementation begins, measurement, including that of capacity, is a tricky business. A good part of the time, it appears to add little to development effectiveness, a pattern in line with some experience in the private sector.[3] Efforts to apply it have the potential to damage the very thing that is being measured. Simply put, measurement can make things worse rather than better. Its application also has a tendency to harm key relationships and spawn a range of bureaucratic dysfunctions ranging from manipulation of the system, to the erection of indicator factories within funding organisations. 'The pressure to act, achieve and count may be overwhelming efforts to understand, analyse and learn' (Wallace and Chapman, Chapter 1).

What is striking is the reluctance in some development circles to think much about the impact of measurement itself. Most donor studies engage in relentless advocacy on its behalf. The focus of the discussion is twofold: first, technique or how to do it better and second, resistance or how to overcome the lack of enthusiasm of those being measured. In its power and simplicity, results measurement appears to its supporters to be an entirely benign type of management intervention without significant side effects. As such, it requires little or no justification. There is little sign in the international development community of the lively debate about the actual value of measurement that can be found easily in the private sector or the education literatures.[4] People who show less than the required level of enthusiasm for measurement are suspected of either resisting change or angling to avoid accountability. And in the process, they are felt to be endangering the credibility of development cooperation.

This chapter looks at this issue from the perspective of development cooperation involving international funding agencies and their partners. It begins with a discussion of the context within which measurement, in general, is undertaken, and then focuses on the downsides and the perverse aspects of the measurement of capacity, more specifically asking: how we can recognise these when they start to appear? The concluding section puts forward some general suggestions about how to improve measurement, by posing a number of questions: What can we do to get the best out of the measurement of capacity while at the same time limiting damage? What is it that makes measurement work effectively? What can we do to promote measurement for development rather than simply the measurement of

---

[3] Neely (2003) estimates that 70 per cent of attempts in the private sector to come up with a 'balanced scorecard' fail.

[4] See Neely (2003). Edward Deming, the father of quality improvement, once declared that 'performance measurement is the most powerful inhibitor to quality and productivity in the Western world'. Quoted in Austin (1996:5). For some of the debate in education circles, see Meier (2002).

development? How can we turn measurement into an effective developmental practice as Taylor and Soal urge?

2.2 The Developmental Context of Measurement

The design and use of measurement systems is now taking place in a development context that has changed considerably over the last two decades. Factors within this context have a major influence on the way some of the key players – international funders, Northern and Southern NGOs, partner governments – go about the practice of performance measurement. We can briefly summarise some of the most obvious factors as follows:

Much development cooperation is now bound by the rules of the performance, measurement and audit culture that has developed in high-income countries over the last two decades. Part of this culture involves rules of the game such as target setting, performance measurement, greater competition and the pervasive use of indicators. Linked to these rules is a perceived need for greater organisational accountability as a means of inducing improved performance. Those both implementing and funding development programmes or projects must increasingly 'demonstrate' results, usually in the short term.

Relationships amongst the participants in many development programmes remain a challenge to get right. Current wisdom tells us that national or local ownership and commitment is perhaps the critical contributor to development effectiveness. Yet most international funding agencies, who are the main proponents of measurement, are structured as cartels with the weight to impose certain key practices on individuals, organisations and governments with whom they work. Furthermore, organisations in low-income countries do not have the capabilities either to measure their own results or even to contest the approaches suggested by external funders. The 'rules of the game' as to who sets the measurement rules, who owns the indicators and who controls the subsequent analysis still remain dominated by the international funding community.

Support for most development interventions in donor countries tends to be uncertain. Many domestic stakeholders are sceptical and intrusive. Bi-lateral donors, in particular, are engaged in a constant search for domestic legitimacy and acceptance. General access to funding seems increasingly fragile and many partner countries and organisations feel the need to compete for resources and attention, as Chapter 1 explains. This sense of competition and financial uncertainty accounts, in part, for the need for development organisations to respond to the latest development fad and fashion, and to the rise of what Wallace and Chapman call 'fear and secrecy' in the aid chain.

Development interventions are now becoming much more complex and varied.

Countries and funders collaborate on huge multi-sectoral programmes including sector-wide approaches and national poverty reduction programmes. They make ambitious efforts to reform whole governments or improve national capacities. In many cases, the accelerating complexity of these efforts is outstripping our attempts to understand them.

Our ways of thinking about measurement are dominated by two perspectives. The first is a deep-seated adherence to a scientific and instrumentalist way of seeing the world. Effectiveness from this perspective comes from the application of technique and procedure. The other is an 'econocratic' perspective that emphasises the power of incentives, markets and individual action to generate progress. The emphasis on human behaviour and values – confidence, resourcefulness, legitimacy – still struggles for attention.

Our understanding of capacity issues is slowly deepening. We know that 'capacity' as a condition or way of being has something to do with skills and resources. But we also realise that the so-called 'softer' issues – confidence, identity, legitimacy, resourcefulness, moral values – also matter a great deal. Moreover, we now know that capacity is not something that can be programmed or planned into existence. It arises from people gaining confidence, shifting their ideas, recrafting their relationships, staking out a protected operating space and above all, learning.

We need to remember that most development interventions take place in the public or non-profit sectors. Many are targeted at activities that are located in these sectors precisely because of measurement difficulties. If their results were so predictable and their benefits so easily attributable, they would likely have been privatised long ago. Causality is hard to establish. The environment is unstable. Multiple contributors enter and leave the scene. Measurement in development is becoming a more difficult exercise. Yet in many cases, the application of measurement techniques for development is becoming more constrained, at the same time as those in the private sector, such as the balanced scorecard, are becoming more flexible and broader in coverage.

2.3 What is Going Wrong? What are the Perverse Effects of Measurement?

The argument that follows is not intended as a contentious rant against the measurement of results itself, nor that specifically associated with capacity. All the issues being addressed – measuring, learning, assessing results – are critical to effective development. People all over the world constantly but informally measure and assess the capacity and performance both of themselves and of their organisations, asking: am I doing well in this job? Does the organisational structure make any sense? Is management leading us in the right direction? Is the efficiency of the financial section going up or down? What does the government think about our work? Everybody acts in their own lives with some intent and expectation of results. All individuals and organisations are, in some way, planning and measuring and assessing and learning.

The connection between results and accountability also makes sense. Anybody engaged in some form of development work needs to be able to ask and answer some basic questions: Are we making a positive difference? Are we helping to create developmental value and for whom? What are we learning about our work and how should we use that learning to improve our contribution? Are we meeting our accountabilities and to whom? Some form of measurement can contribute to answering these questions. The value of collecting useful empirical data also seems obvious. Personal views and anecdotes play a crucial role in the real world, but a systematic effort to supply evidence, data and analysis is also crucial to reaching a reasoned judgement.

The issue under consideration here is the degree to which organisations, especially those embedded in the system of development cooperation, can convert these inherent human abilities into bureaucratised management systems that add some development value. Every devised technique that aims to improve human welfare is contingent. Put simply, it works some of the time for some people on some issues. It provides benefits within a range of conditions and motivations. Outside that range, it is as likely to make things worse as it is to make them better. Efforts at measurement, including that of capacity, can, in practice, behave as virtuous cycles that inject energy and learning into the work of people trying to make things better. The more they add value and the more legitimacy they earn, the more people opt into the system that, in turn, increases energy and learning. Or such systems can go in the other direction and end up as vicious cycles draining motivation, energy and collaboration out of development activities. People exit or ignore the system and in the process, lose the chance to gain and add value.

We need to make every effort to sustain measurement as a positive force for development. But we need to be less complacent about the inherent dangers that come with it. Designing indicators and applying various measurement techniques is the easy part. Turning measurement into a practice that adds real developmental value is the hard part. So where does the measurement of capacity go off track?

There is an Inherent Dynamic to Measure the Wrong Things

This issue of 'mismeasurement' is one of the oldest criticisms of results measurement, but it remains a present problem. Disconnections quickly appear between what is measured and the information that is required or between what is measured and that which is regarded as important. Indicators end up as inaccurate proxies. Measurement thus misses the point in many cases. It tells us about the 'what' and 'when' but much less about the 'how' and the 'why'.

It is, for example, easier to measure the short-term, the tangible, the obvious and the immediate. Inputs and outputs – in many cases in the form of bureaucratic hygiene – lend themselves more easily to measurement. The focus of measurement can also be shaped by the accessibility of data rather than by developmental relevance. But value, quality, inner growth and the slow emergence of systemic changes – in many cases the real determinants of capacity – remain beyond its reach. In some cases, the influence of measurement pushes participants in the process towards both implementing and measuring the obvious and the superficial. Furthermore, participants tend to focus on 'lagging' indicators, meaning those that assess past actions but give relatively little attention to 'leading' indicators, i.e. those that may help to understand future events. Participants start focusing on justifying the past rather than positioning themselves to meet the future.

Another aspect of 'mismeasurement' is the exaggerated focus on indicators. Participants engage in obsessive discussions about indicators, including the 'off-the-shelf' variety devised in a contextual vacuum. They lose track of their significance and start attaching them to every perceived gap and issue. Participants do not decide which are crucial and which are noise. They come to an agreed list of indicators but interpret them using different frameworks and with world views that grant them differing degrees of significance.

Measurement can Lead to Reductionism and Fragmentation

Measurement emphasises a reductionist perspective. Participants tend to focus on disparate aspects of an organisation's capacity and in the process, lose the ability to make a 'systems' judgement. Measurable results that appear to show up in one aspect of the organisation can be undermined by under-reported losses in capacity in other parts. Most measurement approaches do not take into account this kind of system complexity and cost-shifting. Measurement tends to ignore interdependencies while highlighting fragmented gains. In the process, it can reduce the coherence inside the organisation or system. Tight measurement can also lead participants to narrow their field of vision and to miss unintended or unforeseen consequences, some of which will be crucial for capacity development.[5]

---

[5] De Bruijn (2001) cites a remarkable study of the performance of Japanese companies that won the Deming prize for total quality management. For the vast majority of the companies, winning the award was promptly followed by a drop in performance. The explanation appears to lie in their obsessive attention to a few key indicators connected to the prize and their neglect of a wider range of organisational issues. Their tight focus encouraged them to lose track of the constant trade-offs that are involved in any effort to improve capacity and performance.

Measurement: Results inTerms of Development Outcomes rather than Capacity

Most development interventions struggle with the apparent tension between the achievement of substantive outcomes and impacts – the product – and the need to help partners improve their capacity to perform and create value – the process. Indeed, the culture of 'public' activities in both governments and NGOs – their history, incentives, funding systems, patterns of behaviour – have tended to act against sustained attention to capacity development.[6] People and organisations are supposedly rewarded for achieving development outcomes and impacts as the first priority. Creating and nurturing effective organisations is seen as a secondary means.

The point being made here is not that emphases on outcomes and capacity are inherently incompatible: an 'either or' view of the world is increasingly outdated. But moving to a 'both and' perspective is not easy. And the current practice of results measurement is not helping. Substantive results are supposedly tangible and explicit and measurable. Donors, in particular, feel compelled to base their legitimacy on the achievement of product delivery targets rather than the more ephemeral process.[7] Capacity and resourcefulness are, by their very nature, messy conditions to assess. They are characterised by the ambiguous, the intangible and the longer-term. As such, they are difficult to explain or market. Measurement thus tends to aggravate this tension and give more emphasis to a narrower definition of results.

Measurement can Distort Relationships and Behavioural Patterns

Development experience over the last few decades has proven the value of participant commitment, ownership and control. All funders are aware of the disempowering effects of centralised control over programmes and projects. Hierarchical control systems targeted on micro-activities are clearly no longer appropriate or effective. Hence the current shift to less intrusive forms of development relationships usually labelled as partnerships. Yet at the same time, many funders are under enormous domestic pressure to exercise accountability, to demonstrate results and to maintain an appearance of control and purposeful action. In many ways, their own legitimacy and access to continued funding is at stake. Increasingly, this need for accountability is being satisfied through the application of measurement systems which are becoming one of the last mechanisms through which funders can exercise control and accountability.

---

[6] For a discussion of this issue in American NGOs, see Letts et al. (1999).

[7] For an example of one bi-lateral donor, the Netherlands Ministry of Foreign Affairs, addressing this issue, see *Capacity in the Mist*, Proceedings of a subregional workshop on capacity development at Kinigi, Rwanda, October 26–27, 2003.

The application of measurement systems by funders is leading some interventions 'forward towards the past' – the focus on upward accountability, the weakening of trust amongst partners and the erosion of field participant commitment.[8] In many so-called partnerships, measurement is experienced by the less powerful partner as something that increasingly dominates the nature and quality of the relationship. Much of the more nuanced value achieved over time is lost as monitors and evaluators search for results that can be objectively verified. In response to the resulting loss of trust, field participants begin to take compensatory, defensive action in the form of opting out or gaming the system. Donors set the rules of the measurement game but field participants play it. The more one group tries to capture and control the measurement system, the less effective it becomes. In the process, measurement ceases to be an integral part of ongoing cycles of purposeful action. It gets disconnected from the critical internal learning processes that lie at the heart of effective development. Measurement ends up as a detached system extracting information out of the participants who themselves are trapped in a web of administrative processes with little or no context. A 'tragedy of the measurement commons' can evolve in which all the actors end up worse off for their efforts. The measurement system loses credibility and energy and enters a downward spiral. The process proceeds to undermine the very condition – enhanced capacity – that it was designed to support.

Measurement can Quickly Deteriorate into a Form of Symbolic Ritual

One of the most obvious dangers is emergence of symbolism.[9] Many participants are under external pressure to 'demonstrate' results. The underlying use of measurement becomes one of protecting the interests of the participants at all levels. Measurement soon leads to excessive documentation, illusionary formal reports, symbolic images and Potemkin-village indicators. What matters most is the appearance of things – improving indicators, the apparent existence of a functioning measurement system, the apparent commitment of the participants to results. In many cases, this resort to symbolic ritual is a much more rational option in terms of organisational survival than following the arduous path of real capacity and performance. Participants are more likely to be rewarded for symbolic, if illusionary, achievements than for recording an honest but failed attempt at genuine performance. Participants supply the measures but not the sustained results. The system, in effect, acts to buffer the operating space and access to resources of the participants. Everybody ends up with an interest in perpetuating a system that is producing meagre developmental benefits. Technical rationalists may wince at this

---

[8] For the same phenomenon in the UK, see O'Neill (2002).

[9] cf. Dar, Chapter 4.

scenario, but it does explain, at least in part, the pervasive lack of operational impact of most performance measurement systems.

Measurement is Turning into a Substitute for a Capacity Development Strategy

Part of the current appeal of results measurement is its attractiveness – by itself – as a capacity development strategy. According to this view, the very existence of targets and indicators can create a 'demand' for capacity. The simple act of focusing staff attention on performance can cause them to try and improve it. The specification of results will act as a magnet pulling and aligning activities in the right direction through the sheer power of incentives and accountability. This is the 'iron filings' perspective of capacity development. Much of the old-style 'supply-side' interventions in support of results – learning, thinking through strategies, conscious experimentation, building skills, confidence and awareness – can then be given less attention. Demand-side approaches with their accompanying indicators of progress have an important contribution to make. But they can lead quickly to a form of development accounting. They also tip over into dysfunction when participants mix up demand, need and opportunity. Attention to the 'what' needs to be supplemented with an understanding of the 'how' coming from the supply side. We need both sides – the demand and the supply – coming together.

Measurement can Bias Development Efforts against Innovation and Experimentation

A tension has always existed between the 'planning' view of capacity development emphasising structure, targeting, clarity and prediction and the 'adaptive' view which gives more value to experimentation, discovery and an openness to unforeseen circumstances. The logframe is the symbol of the first. Process approaches are the signature of the second. In practice, the urge to measure aligns itself most comfortably with the planning view. A pattern of desired results is selected and participants are tasked with achieving them. A bias develops against questioning the pattern. Few incentives exist for welcoming the unexpected or unforeseen which, in most cases, are the most revealing. Reporting styles in particular focus on 'single loop' learning in which progress against pre-set targets is emphasised. Participants have to calculate carefully the inclination of the key stakeholders to see innovation and creativity as deviations from agreed objectives. Measurement systems start 'freezing' and act against adaptation.

Measurement Systems get Trapped in the Paradox of Time versus Deterioration

Many results measurement systems need time to develop. This applies in particular to capacity issues, a good number of which are resistant to rapid change. Early attempts at measurement usually produce data that is notoriously unreliable and misleading. Most approaches need three to five years before their behaviours are institutionalised, the right indicators have emerged and the longer-term trends in capacity are evident. But measurement systems tend to deteriorate over time and many organisations do not have the infrastructure or the skills to sustain the long march to effective measurement. They are not properly structured or resourced to support implementation. They sink under the weight of indicator design, data collection, report writing and negotiations with funders. Efforts at measurement lose focus. People get tired and fed up with the meagre benefits after the initial outlay of energy. Funders and participating organisations opt out of the system and pass on the costs of measurement to individuals who have many others tasks. The system loses energy and relevance over time and tips over into symbolic compliance just as it should be reaching the point of greater effectiveness.

2.4 So What to Do?

If these perverse effects of measurement keep reappearing, the following questions arise: are these the results of poor implementation which can supposedly be corrected by improved technique? Or are we dealing here with generic flaws and contradictions in the practice of measurement that can only be managed rather than resolved? We are unlikely to rely on improved technique *by itself* to make the measurement of capacity effective. We should give up our fixation with finding the perfect indicators. In the end, the key to effective measurement will lie in the values and motivations of the participants – their willingness to learn, and to confront themselves, their openness and their integrity in pursuit of developmental value. These qualities will, in turn, be fostered by the creation of learning communities that themselves can push forward with effective measurement and with capacity development itself.

Listed below are eight general principles to improve the measurement of capacity. More specific techniques are omitted given their analysis in many other reports and documents.[10]

1. Participants need to develop some sort of shared working understanding of the concept of capacity.
One of the first things is to come to some sort of shared understanding in any development intervention about what it is we think we are measuring. What do we mean by the term 'capacity'? Are we talking about conventional organisational and technical capacities such as fundraising or advocacy or service delivery? Or are we

---

[10] See for example Horton et al. (2003).

talking about intangibles such as confidence and identity? Or tangibles such as physical or financial resources? Are we talking about individual or organisation-wide capacities? Are we dealing with generic capacities such as the intellectual? Are we talking about different combinations of capacities for different types of organisations at different stages of their evolution?[11] Or are we talking about 'capabilities' in the sense used by Amartya Sen (1999)? And should we focus on existing capacities and strengths or their absence or gaps?

We do not suggest any particular categorisation in this chapter. But we do support any approach that encourages participants to think through answers to these questions and arrive over time at some sort of shared understanding.[12]

2. We need to approach the measurement of capacity from a different direction.

We cannot simply apply the conventional approaches to measurement that may be used to assess outputs and outcomes in other parts of a programme. Indeed, those approaches themselves appear to be falling short in less ambiguous circumstances. We need to shift our mindset to one that is more flexible, curious, experimental, and inclusive. Informal methods matter more. Trust amongst the participants becomes crucial. Continuous dialogue and experimentation must get more emphasis. There must be more tolerance for looking at capacity issues from different angles. Subjectivity becomes legitimate. The field of vision – the context – and the length of vision – the time frame – expand. Much of the insight that matters comes from converting the tacit shared knowledge of the participants into explicit knowledge that can lead to action.

We intuitively know that many of the ways we used to make sense of the world no longer serve us well. We know that reductionist ways of thinking – breaking the capacity 'machine' up into pieces – and then trying to put it back together tell us little. We suspect that most of the tools and frameworks we use in development cooperation – logical frameworks, work breakdown structures, results chains, input/output models – are not getting us very far, especially with respect to the dreaded 'why' question. But what are busy practitioners to do? Where are the tools

---

[11] One report that addresses this issue of capacity identification directly is that of the International Forum on Capacity Building. See their publication *Capacity Building of Southern NGOs*, www.ifcb-ngo.org

[12] There is a good deal of experience set out in the private sector literature that shows a similar process of thinking specifically about the concept of capacity. It may not be directly applicable but it does point the way to new insights that might be of use to development practitioners. See Salaman and Asch (2003); Lynch et al. (2003); Sanchez (2001); Dubois (1993); Hodgkinson and Sparrow (2002); Yeung et al. (1999); Garratt (2000); Somerville and Mroz (1997); Jenster and Hussey (2001); and Dubois (1998).

for the new century? Many already exist. Much has been written on systems thinking, some of which is now slowly making its way into the somewhat insular world of development cooperation.[13] Our challenge is to use these new approaches to think differently about issues such as capacity.

3. We need to re-balance the relationship between the measurement of capacity and the measurement of performance.

The usual approach in most development interventions is to set programme or performance goals and then to analyse the capacity 'gaps' or constraints that hinder the achievement of those goals.[14] Performance outcomes and impacts are a higher order or the real ends of any intervention. They can and should be measured separately. Capacity is the means and can also be assessed independently. And yet it makes as much sense to reverse or at least re-balance this perspective. Programmes come and go. Priorities change and shift. But helping a group or an organisation or a society to create and recreate its capacity to perform must also be an ultimate goal or end. Achieving outcomes and impacts remains an end but also must be seen as a means. Capacity is in many ways the potential to perform. It can be demonstrated partly by the emergence of performance. But performance has limited long-term value if it is not used to strengthen capacity. The measurement of each must be intertwined and interrelated.

Our friends in the private sector understand this point better than we do in the public or NGO sectors. For firms and corporations, the effectiveness of the organisation – its capacity – is critical for commercial and financial survival. Arie de Gues (1997:6) talks about senior management's top concern and priority being the health of the institution as a whole. Collins and Porras (1994) see 'clock-building' and not 'time telling' as the key to sustainable leadership.[15]

4. Any effort to assess capacity must be tied to a similar effort to assess how capacity will develop.

Many development interventions come with well-defined goals, objectives, missions and indicators of anticipated capacity – the 'what' stuff that fits well within the measurement framework. These aspects move more to the rhythms of funder

---

[13] See Wheatley and Kellner-Rogers (1996). Also Rihani (2001).

[14] 'GEF views capacity development interventions primarily as functional means towards more substantive ends, global environmental benefits...Up to this point, it has not been possible to design and develop projects focused primarily or solely on developing capacity' quoted in Furtado (2003:4).

[15] They note that, 'The continual stream of great products and services from highly visionary companies stems from them being outstanding organisations, not the other way around' Collin and Porras (1994).

procedures and policies such as the project cycle and much less in line with the inherent natural cycle of developmental processes. But we frequently do not understand much about the dynamics of complex social, organisational and institutional change. We end up clear about the future but uncertain about the present or the past. And in the process, we make assumptions about 'capacity' – what it is and how to support its emergence and what to measure – that are largely untenable. We need to learn more about how and why capacity 'systems' operate and what patterns of interest and benefits lock them into place. In other words, we need to use measurement to deepen our understanding and to learn much more about how change happens.

5. The assessment of capacity is a collective shared endeavour. The behaviour of the participants has to be encouraged to reflect that goal.

The measurement of capacity for the most part has been treated as an apolitical, acultural technique that needs further refining to be effective. In the process, we have given too little attention to the critical question about its implications for human behaviour: how will people in this situation react when their results are measured? Will the validity of the information produced by the measurement system be compromised by the likely reactions of those being measured? Who owns the measurement system and what is their agenda? Who stands to gain – and lose – from measurement and under what conditions? How can we design the system in a way that encourages the collaboration and shared efforts that are crucial to its effectiveness? What else needs to be done to encourage participants to use the measurement system for productive purposes?

Measurement thus takes its place as the latest in a long line of development efforts that bump up against unforeseen behavioural consequences. In many cases, measurement both responds and contributes to a series of perverse incentives which encourage the participants at all levels to adopt defensiveness as a strategy. People are instinctively wary about the intent of bureaucratic systems. They need some incentives and some reassurance about their actual use. Any measurement system should therefore be based on a deep knowledge of the culture and behavioural patterns of a particular organisation. And we need better understandings about the use to which measurement will be put and by whom. We are still struggling to find approaches to measurement which consistently encourage courage and openness. In the end, the success of measurement circles back to depend on the quality of relationships and the level of trust and fairness that guide the work.

6. Participants, including funders, must invest in the organisational capabilities needed for the effective measurement of capacity.

As mentioned earlier, many programmes invest heavily in the production of the outputs of measurement systems – the endless reports, the data gathering, the monitoring visits, the endless discussion about indicators. But they tend to invest relatively little in building the capabilities, both individual and organisational, that are needed to sustain the system. These systems face a whole series of constraints to implementation – technical, organisational, political, social, financial and cultural. Different groups at different levels need the resources, operating space, reassurance and incentives to maintain their involvement. And a culture of honesty and integrity needs to be encouraged that rewards openness and acts against opting out or manipulation.

The obvious questions arise. Have we thought enough about the design and management of the measurement process as opposed to its outputs? Have participants at different levels thought about it? How is this process actually going to work? And do we understand how it fits with the existing informal pattern of measuring, assessing and learning?

7. We need to recognise and manage the tensions amongst the purposes of measurement.

Any approach to measurement contains a variety of objectives. It must help to maintain accountability. It must contribute to learning and better management. It must help to motivate staff. It must be used for demonstration purposes to reassure stakeholders. Yet we also know that these various objectives can come with inherent contradictions. Funding agencies use measurement to demonstrate accountability only to be faced with the costs of declining learning and participant commitment. Measures designed for collecting objective information lead to the demotivation of the key groups and individuals within the organisation. Field participants hoard information to maintain their credibility only to lose the support of their funders. Focusing tightly on key indicators in the name of measurement validity lowers rather than improves the level of overall performance. A measurement system designed to help delegate authority based on clear accountabilities ends up re-centralising authority. Techniques designed to promote more efficiency act instead to undermine existing capacity.

When it comes to developing capacity, the only way out of this dilemma is to make a clear choice for action learning and self-management as the underlying objectives. Indeed without that choice, real accountability is not possible. The measurement system tips over again into dysfunction which cannot be remedied by hierarchical control. This chapter is not the place to elaborate on recent advances in the promotion of learning within the practice of development cooperation. But there are some encouraging signs of progress in this area and more sustained attention needs to be given to it in the interests of improving the impact of measurement.[16]

---

[16] See Carlsson and Wohlgemuth (2000), and Roper et al. (2003).

8. Place the function of measurement in a broader context of assessment, learning and sense-making.
We need to place the function of the measurement of capacity into a broader context of analysis, dialogue, reflection, feedback, decisions and action. Part of the dreary legacy of the logframe has been to frame some results analysis as a kind of development crossword puzzle that can be solved by filling in the boxes. Measurement can help us build an understanding about complex phenomena such as capacity and capacity development. It can encourage the use of evidence and empirical data. It can push people to subject their thinking to scrutiny. It can inform dialogue and reflection. It can become a key part of a larger process of assessment and learning. But more is needed. What else do participants need to do in addition to measurement to understand their circumstances?

Two things appear to matter. The first is the issue of sense making. We know that indicators by themselves tell us little about issues such as capacity. Data from indicators raise more questions than they resolve. Indicators act as 'can openers' rather than 'dials'. Wenger (1998: Ch. 8) writes about organisations using stories to help explain context and causality.[17] Such an approach also helps to build the culture that values innovation and knowledge sharing. The second crucial issue is the formation of some sort of fora for discussion and action that can facilitate collective learning and a shared understanding. Communities of practice, knowledge communities and informal networks can all encourage these processes. Such connections can also help link the development of knowledge to those who can apply it.[18]

2.5 Summary

We return to our original question: is the measurement of capacity still a good idea? The view in this chapter is a qualified *yes*, provided we broaden the way we think and act. In particular we need to do three things. First, we need to see capacity, in the form of much more effective individuals, groups and organisations, as perhaps the most critical development result. And we need to think of measurement as a key contribution in terms of helping to create that result. Second, we need to admit that we are all collectively at the early stages of knowing how to turn measurement into good development practice. The most promising approaches lie scattered in countless locations and experiences around the world ranging from small NGOs in some of the world's poorest countries to some of the more

---

[17] See also Denning (2001).

[18] For a discussion of this point, see Engel et al. (2003).

61

advanced techniques being tried out in major consulting firms in high-income countries. Bringing these together in ways that can be accessible to practitioners remains a challenge. And third, we need to act individually with integrity and openness. In the end, the insistence of people at all levels of the development enterprise to support collective learning and positive action as the goals of measurement will make the crucial difference.

CHAPTER 3

Rights, Culture and Contested Modernities

David Marsden

3.1 Introduction

We are at a crossroads in our thinking about development. The instruments that we have traditionally used to achieve an evolving set of policy objectives and sustainable development outcomes are no longer adequate. Old certainties and established methods are being questioned. A reflexive awareness is changing the ways in which we view the development task. Ideas about progress are changing, as achievements are questioned. Debates between those who favour growth and those who favour equity divide the development community. The mono-cultural, neo-liberal development model is challenged by movements of cultural and economic resistance. New forms of engagement are being explored. Most aid agencies are struggling to establish different sorts of relationships with their Southern and Eastern 'partners'. Civil society organisations are encouraged to challenge established arrangements. Government agencies are encouraged to move from being the deliverers of goods and services, to being facilitators; the midwives of an emergent society focused on including and empowering the poor. This shift from the delivery of outputs to the achievement of outcomes implies a fundamental shift in the ways in which we view and evaluate 'development interventions'.

We need a thorough evaluation of the strategies, approaches and methods that we have adopted in the past. The traditional, externally conceived and imposed development model does not help when we wish to understand how participation, social capital, partnerships, empowerment, local ownership, capacity or human rights are engendered. Indeed, if we genuinely wish to build civic-driven development,[1] we need seriously to address what it is and what we can do.

We need to question some of the presumptions that underpin the often positivist and instrumentalist perspectives that have monopolised explanations and policy discussions. Development thinking is still dominated by presumptions that *they have problems that we can fix*. Positivism and instrumentalism inform a linear approach to problem solving. This is enshrined in such things as 'the project cycle' and 'the logical framework'.[2] The aim is to achieve consensus about direction and progress through rationalist discourse on the basis of evidence from experts.

There is a continued concern with the inadequacy of this instrumental and mechanistic view of the world. Despite the rhetoric of participation and the emphasis on empowerment and institutional and capacity development, most donor activities are still driven by presumptions about the timely and more cost effective delivery of goods and services. Development discourse is still (and arguably increasingly) dominated by notions of efficiency, calculability, predictability and control. The assumptions that we need more and better targeted aid still inform the practice of a large majority of development professionals.

We need to examine the premises that underpin the old ways of seeing – the 'world views' that still inform much development thinking. One way of doing this is by focusing on 'rights-based' approaches to development, as opposed to 'needs-based' approaches. This is not to suggest that we pursue one or the other, but rather that we see the latter as encompassed by the former – as we recognise the need to tackle the root causes, rather than just the symptoms of poverty (Thin 2002). The shift in focus is much more than just a shift from the delivery of goods and services to the development of collaborative and supportive partnerships. It marks the beginnings of a fundamental realignment of actors and resources. It points to the re-establishment of the 'social', following an era dominated by the 'individual'; the re-establishment of economic, social and cultural rights after the legalistic preoccupation with civil and political rights. It raises questions about 'hard' versus 'soft' law, about the place of customary law, about the enforceability of codes of conduct and the establishment and maintenance of minimum standards and their

---

[1] I use 'civic-driven development' as opposed to 'community-driven development' because it highlights the many different groups and interests present within communities, and focuses on values, and the pursuit of rights, inherent in the development of civil society. I am grateful to Alan Fowler for pointing out this important difference.

[2] See Biggs and Smith (2002) in which they challenge the importance given to PCM (Project Cycle Management) tools and techniques.

replication.

3.2 Culture

In tackling these issues and re-establishing the space for social development it is essential to put the study of 'culture' at the very heart of our enquiry. Culture is not just another variable to be taken into account, not an extra to be added to an already complicated agenda. Culture is at the heart of all development models and all development models are cultural, whether they emanate from Brussels, Washington, Dushanbe, Dhaka or Beijing.

Focusing on culture opens up the debate about values and, within that debate, about evaluation, the negotiation of value and calculability. It raises some of the dilemmas surrounding universal rights and relative values enshrined in different cultural traditions. It raises questions about the interpretations of culture in a world where no culture can be deemed 'traditional' and where the very notion of culture associated with ethnic identity is subject to rapid evolution and often violent contests. Indeed contested cultural interpretations occupy the major interfaces between different understandings of the pathways to development. Focusing on culture also raises questions about the explicit or implicit value judgements and cultural biases that are often inherent in supposedly 'neutral', 'objective', and 'value free' approaches and methodologies.

Culture has traditionally been defined in terms of the past – traditions, heritage, customs and habits. As such it has often been perceived as an obstacle to development. Development is about the future – about plans, targets, goals, and hopes. Anthropology has traditionally been concerned with the preservation of this past heritage. Economics, by contrast, has been concerned with the future (Appadurai 2004). It comes as no surprise to learn that it was anthropologists who opposed the ratification of the Universal Declaration of Human Rights some fifty years ago, steeped as many were then in cultural relativist thinking. The pursuit of civil and political rights appeared to supersede and override the rights to separate identities enshrined in 'traditional cultures'.

Closing down or opening up?

The tensions between anthropology and economics arising from these different orientations are still being played out in debates, for example, about the rights of indigenous peoples. They are also manifest at a wider level in terms of the struggle over definitions about what is indigenous,[3] and over the authority of customary law and customary rights. Current practice focuses on 'closing down' and narrow-

---

[3] Indigenous peoples are still being 'discovered': in 1992 a national census in Chile showed that a greater percentage of the population was of Mapuche origin than had hitherto been acknowledged. See INTRAC: *Ontrac* No. 23, January 2003. www.intrac.org

ly circumscribing the definitions of particular indigenous people, rather than recognising that the establishment of differences is part of the development of relationships, however antagonistic these may turn out to be. A recognition of the importance of difference and of the value of *dissensus*[4] gives us space to examine the processes of evolution of relationships and positions. Closing down, on the other hand, implies tighter and narrower definitions and more comprehensive mapping and surveying of activities and relationships – the imposition of a particular perception of the world surrounding, for example, the expansion of private property rights, or the collectivisation of agriculture during the Soviet era. The implications of this are explored more thoroughly in the work of James Scott (1997; 1998), for example. At an even more general level this imposition is still reflected in the struggles between social development and economic development, and between the role of the state, the role of civil society, and the role of the market. On the one hand there are attempts to understand that result in greater control and predictability, on the other there are attempts to understand that aim to liberate and to celebrate diversity and ambiguity.

Appadurai (2004) provides us with three building blocks or principles with which to approach the incorporation of a cultural perspective more centrally. First, recognise that cultural coherence is not a matter of individual items, but of their relationships ('north' is only understandable in terms of 'south', 'indigenous' is only understandable in relationship to 'exogenous'); elements make sense only in terms of their relationships.[5] Second, recognise that *dissensus* is an integral part of culture. Third, recognise that the boundaries of cultural systems are very leaky and that mutations take place; cultures are heterogeneous, diverse and plural. These three building blocks are analogous to those that support an organic worldview outlined by the physicist Fritjof Capra, who identifies social organisations as living organisms.

In an attempt to bring the future into a study of culture, Appadurai (2004) introduces the concept of 'aspiration'. This includes an analysis of how 'collective horizons' are shaped and how peoples' aspirations are translated into wants, preference, choices and calculations. How they relate to others in their pursuit of sustainable livelihood strategies. Cultivating this capacity to aspire among the poor is at the heart of any strategy to empower. The pursuit of a rights-based approach to development focuses on these aspirations. Rights are then claims on the future, the foundations on which the struggles for dignity, equity and justice can be built:

...culture is a dialogue between aspirations and sedimented traditions. And in

---

[4] The term *dissensus* is used to suggest a lack of consensus, rather than outright discord or dissent.

[5] This is the essence of a reflexive awareness.

our commendable zeal for the latter at the cost of the former, we have allowed an unnecessary, harmful and artificial opposition to emerge between culture and development. By bringing the future back in, by looking at aspirations as cultural capabilities, we are surely in a better position to understand how people actually navigate their social spaces. And, in terms of the relationship between democracy and development, this approach gives us a principled reason to build the capacity to aspire in those who have the most to lose from its underdevelopment – the poor themselves.[6]

3.3 Context

Another central element in the struggle to give meaning is 'context'. Context opens up the debate about the use of indigenous concepts and institutions, and the construction of local solutions. It provides an opportunity to argue for the central importance of historical and thus contextual understanding. The demise of the Soviet Union may have ultimately discredited a particular brand of socialism associated with a particular type of regime, but it did not end the struggle between the individual and the communal or collective that has been such a feature of development debates over the past century.

The 'context' of the changing nature of the nation state, the significance of processes of globalisation, the roles of individuals and collectivities, the negotiations between different groups, provide the arenas in which new relationships are cultivated, new partnerships are built, new cultures are created and new enemies identified. A rights-based approach, together with the increased attention given to the environment, and the empowerment of the poor, allows us to begin to focus again more clearly on particular groups within society. Some of this is, of course, not new; concerns with child rights, gender imbalances, and indigenous peoples, for example, have already received significant attention, and arguably provide the bases on which wider struggles for equity and justice are now based. Some of it dates back to the great ideological divides that separated capitalism from socialism. But it does allow us to see a little more clearly beyond the public and formal faces of communities usually presented to us by élites and agents of the formal institutions of government with whom we most commonly interface. It allows us to bring politics back into the debate with the re-affirmation that there is no neutral ground. It also allows us to re-visit the concerns that underpinned thinking about (and the growth of) social development and emerging concerns with the environment perhaps three or four decades ago.

A focus on context also raises questions about replicability and the 'scaling up'

---

[6] Appadurai (2004). Extract is from July 2001 Draft: 19.

and transfer of approaches and methodologies from one place to another. It raises fundamental questions about the nature and types of engagement and the time periods and horizons associated with that engagement. As we begin to understand the implications of a 'network society' (Castells 1996) in an era of global communications, 'virtual' communities become central to building capacity, developing organisations and exchanging knowledge. As we try to internalise the processes associated with 'putting the last first', the importance of building 'learning organisations' and constructing innovative alliances, we recognise the need for long-term engagements with partners we can trust.

We are slowly cultivating a more reflexive awareness of our roles as development professionals, in the processes of 'globalisation' as they unfold in local contexts. This means deploying more inductive rather than deductive and reductive reasoning and moving beyond the mechanistic paradigm that emerged with the works of Descartes and Newton and that has underpinned and defined our thinking since the seventeenth century. It means questioning the 'McDonaldisation' of the world (Ritzer 1996) based on Taylorian principles of scientific management. This is one of the main obstacles to organisational change as Capra (2002) asserts in his latest work, *The Hidden Connections*. We are only now beginning to appreciate the complexities of the different realities with which we choose to engage and of the multiple networks that we construct and in which we are embedded.

Worldviews and Metaphors

We need to recognise that the mechanistic paradigm is only one, albeit powerful, way of seeing the world. It is a metaphor of how we perceive order.[7] In the industrial machine age it underpinned our concerns with achieving efficiency, calculability, predictability and control. It supported the pursuit of increased productivity and our notions of economic growth. It underpinned the development of scientific disciplines and was the cornerstone of economic thought. It was also responsible for severe social and political disruptions associated, first with the enclosure movement, then with the growth of the factory, mechanisation and attendant social and economic inequalities.

But there are other metaphors that inform our ways of thinking and seeing and thus of acting on the world. In the literature on management they are elegantly elaborated by Gareth Morgan. In wider cultural terms of course these metaphors inform the world views of all social groups. They form the building blocks on which anthropologists have built their discipline and the world views that inform that evolving discipline.

---

[7] As Morgan (1997:4) notes, 'The use of metaphor implies a way of thinking and a way of seeing that pervade how we understand our world generally'.

One powerful metaphor that has gained increasing credence over the past 25 years or so is that of social organisations as complex living organisms constantly evolving and changing. This has its roots in increasing concerns with ecology and with the natural environment, and with the place of human societies within it. It places greater value on relationships between 'things' than on the 'things' themselves. Capra (2002: 100) argues that 'understanding human organisations as living systems is one of the critical challenges of our time'. He understands social organisations as having a dual nature. They are designed for particular purposes and at the same time they are composed of groups of people who build relationships and interact. In other words they are the formal designed structures and informal networks that resist design. We often only see the designed structures. Unless we gain deeper understandings we miss the informal networks and relationships where the 'living' takes place. As Capra puts it 'the designed structure always intersects with the organisation's living individuals and communities, for whom change cannot be designed' (Ibid: 99). For Capra it is the relationships and interactions within and between people in organisations where *life* and the *spirit* of community lies. Such 'networking' has changed the ways in which we build coalitions and leverage influence.

Communities of Practice

It is through these networks that knowledge and information, the life-blood of organisations, flow. Etienne Wenger, an organisational theorist, writing about 'learning as a social system' (and focused on management within organisations), stresses the key importance of knowledge (Wenger 1998; Wenger et al. 2002). Traditionally, we have seen knowledge as something to be captured and put into libraries or knowledge banks. And yet we have little knowledge about how to create and leverage it in practice. Databases and libraries remain lifeless until they are used by individuals, groups and networks in the pursuit of goals and objectives. The transfer of knowledge does not guarantee its effective use. Knowledge is not the asset or the capital – people are. Measuring the effectiveness of training programmes for example has proved notoriously difficult using traditional tools and techniques. How do we know when capacity has been developed?

Perhaps we are asking the wrong questions? Perhaps we should be focusing on the dynamics that connect these groups and networks, the relationships that give meaning to the elements connected, and the conditions that are needed to facilitate their development? Rather than seeing knowledge as made up of discrete elements, or bits of information, packaged and codified in particular ways, we should be reading between the lines of their production and examining the culturally informed and informal dynamics of its production and its application in particular contexts.

Wenger's concept of 'communities of practice' provides one way of approaching this subject. He defines communities of practice as 'groups of people who share a concern, a set of problems, or a passion about a topic, and who deepen their knowledge and expertise in this area by interacting on an ongoing basis' (Wenger et al. 2002: 4). These communities of practice have three characteristics: (a) mutual engagement in a joint enterprise; (b) a shared repertoire of knowledge and routines; and (c) tacit rules of conduct (Wenger 1998: 72ff). Capra maintains that an 'organisation's *aliveness* resides in its communities of practice' (Capra 2002: 109). Focusing on communities of practice allows us to look at the ways in which these informal networks and associations interact with the formal structures within and between which they operate.

We can lose this focus when we talk of 'communities' in terms of geographically distinct units – villages, hamlets and neighbourhoods – and fail to examine the inter-locking 'communities of practice' contained within those villages. Many geographical communities, like business organisations, are established for particular purposes by outsiders, and bring together groups from different places with different backgrounds and different interests. Many of the newer settlements in Central Asia, for example, involved the involuntary settlement and resettlement of nomads and people from different regions to work on newly opened-up irrigated land. They often spoke different languages and held different interests. With the demise of the former Soviet Union, the need to retain the formal production structure changed. The result in Tajikistan was civil war. Attempts to focus on *community-driven development* that is based on geography and the assumptions of common interest will only reproduce the inequitable and exploitative social hierarchies that were prevalent in the Soviet era, and on which many irrigation systems are ultimately based.

The example from Central Asia shows how focusing on communities of practice provides a tool for getting beyond the formal structures that define relationships between people, that codify rules and regulations and more importantly articulate power relations. It opens up the informal networks for analysis and support – the tacit knowledge that is created and resides in organisations and is often hidden and unspoken. This has been variously described as social capital, a commodity like any other form of capital, or as 'trust' which by its very nature cannot be reduced to a commodity, and whose essence lies in its 'between-ness'.

A word of caution at this point however is necessary. These informal networks are the repositories of cultures of resistance as well as the well springs of creativity. They may also reinforce existing inequalities through the preservation of networks of privilege and 'underground' or 'illegal' forms of association.[8] If the objective of management is perceived as capturing, co-opting and controlling them, as it is presumably with illicit associations and those that work against man-

---

[8] For an earlier discussion of the management of knowledge, see Marsden (1994).

agement prescriptions, then strategies of resistance are likely to be forthcoming (Scott 1997; 1998; Cooke and Kothari 2001). These strategies of resistance may emerge within organisations, with strikes, go-slows, theft or deliberate subversion. They may emerge within social groups through deliberate strategies to undermine or circumvent formal systems of control by withholding information, non-collaboration or deliberate sabotage.

If, on the other hand, the role of management is seen as empowering and including these communities of practice, there is a recognition that 'the most effective way to enhance an organisation's potential for creativity and learning, to keep it vibrant and alive, is to support and strengthen its communities of practice' (Capra 2002: 111). These are often found at the peripheries or on the borders of organisations. Strategies for building 'partnerships' will need to tread a fine line between temptations to co-opt and impose and efforts to liberate and expose. The evolving lives of these communities of practice will necessarily involve a struggle between these two opposing interests – the need for structure and order and the need for change and evolution. If we recognise Appadurai's second building block – that cultures are characterised by *dissensus* as well as consensus – then organisations, whether they are water user groups or private sector production companies, will always contain (contradictory) tendencies for both opening up and closing down, in terms of whether they are struggling to maintain order or struggling to break free from constraints. For the development practitioner the critical question centres around which forces she will ally herself with. The answer to that question will necessarily involve moral and ethical choices and cannot be answered solely by recourse to an instrumentalist prescription about the delivery of goods and services.

Again the case of former Soviet Central Asia provides a useful example. During the Soviet period many systems for water use were installed in villages in Central Asia. These are now falling into disrepair and need upgrading. Users treat water as a free good and as a commodity supplied by the state. New projects, financed by external donors, to rehabilitate old systems are often predicated on building local ownership and on encouraging people to pay for upkeep and maintenance. The old thinking assumes that the state will continue to provide, and political capital is gained by promises of provision. New donors, however, insist on building community-driven and pro-poor strategies that challenge the established order. The question then is to what extent is it possible to challenge the existing order by insisting on reforms, and defying established arrangements and institutions.

Dealing with change then means recognising that solutions are emergent within particular cultural contexts in terms of the interactions between formal institutions and communities of practice. Culture and context emerge as the most important explanatory variables in any examination of the tensions between the formal institutions that regulate the distribution of power, and the informal communities of practice seeking to build sustainable livelihood strategies. The use of the term

71

sustainable livelihood strategies here is deliberate. Members of communities of practice, who control the distribution of resources associated with the flow of development funds, through patronage networks, or other corrupt means, are also engaged in building what they might regard as sustainable livelihoods.

Measurement

The tensions between formal institutions and the rules and regulations embodied in them, and the informal communities of practice, emerge in issues surrounding measurement and performance. One particular aspect of this tension is manifest in the debates surrounding quantitative and qualitative measurements and the relative merits surrounding their use.[9] Another particular aspect of the tension is between the search for meaningful results, through results-based management practices, and quality assurance measures, on the one hand, and the freedom to experiment and involve stakeholders in processes with often unpredictable outcomes. I would argue that much of the debate revolves around trying to compare apples with oranges. More than that, perhaps, we are trying to use a mechanistic metaphor to explore what can only fruitfully be explored using a totally different metaphor, that of a living system. Switching between metaphors, or 'ways of seeing' and 'ways of thinking', requires rather different questions to be posed and fundamentally different perceptions about measurement to be introduced. As Johnson, who started his career as an accountant, has argued, 'The practice of measurement leads, over time, to reductionist thinking and then to mechanistic activity – which does an incredible job of destroying nature and the natural sensibility' (Johnson 1999).

We cannot 'measure' empowerment, sustainability, inclusion, capacity development, the achievements of rights-based approaches, or even social capital, if we cling to the mechanical model. While traditional forms of analysis can be extended to these new sets of problems, they are unlikely to provide us with anything more than activity-based measures.

When measurement becomes a tool for fragmenting our understanding, and assessing one process, or one person, as better than another on some objective scale, then it is inherently unnatural. Accountants and economists regularly operate in this unnatural manner, and when it fails to predict the world's behavior accurately, they refine and redefine the mathematics in their models. But to paraphrase Bateson, describing the world through any mechanistic set of measurements is like partaking of a meal by eating the menu (Ibid: 291).

---

[9] See proceedings from workshops held at Cornell and at Swansea – for a link to the Cornell workshop proceedings go to www.people.cornell.edu/pages/sk145. For a link to the Swansea workshop visit www.swan.ac.uk/cds/research/SDRC/conference_on_combining_qualitat.htm

This is not about seeing qualitative and quantitative methods as though they were two ends of a spectrum and assuming that richer explanations will emerge from a judicious mix between the two. Those assumptions are essentially based on an unreflexive and linear form of enquiry.

The Organic Metaphor

We structure reality by the ways in which we view it and the metaphors that we deploy to understand it. As Morgan (1997) points out, each metaphor is partial and hides some aspects; in fore-grounding some forms of interpretation it backgrounds others. Arguably the mechanical metaphor has run its course and the organic metaphor is gaining in ascendancy. We need to recognise that meanings are negotiated and that our actions are implicitly if not explicitly informed by particular and often competing world views. These emanate from particular cultural contexts. Both the mechanistic and the organic metaphors are creations of the West. Their recognition and interpretation by or applicability to other parts of the world will be integral to the negotiation of meaning in the pursuit of progress. The organic metaphor, however, seems to permit an easier incorporation of diversity, inter-connectedness and justice in our relationships with others and with the natural environment.

The shift from projects to programmes, and from aid donors to 'partners' in development is one dimension of this change in world view. The traditional focus on projects is being replaced by a more holistic and comprehensive focus on programmes and on processes. We recognise that we cannot treat even large scale physical engineering projects as *merely* engineering projects. The construction of dams, for example, is intimately bound up with the visions of development that people espouse and the dynamics of relationships, interpretations and alliances that people are able to construct. The sites of proposed dams are sites for contested views of modernity and exist in particular cultural contexts that need to be unpacked and situated.

A concomitant shift towards a more organic way of seeing is also to be found in the current emphasis on outcomes rather than outputs and manifests itself in the struggle to build frameworks that support integration (Comprehensive Development Frameworks) and approaches that are pro-poor (Poverty Reduction Strategy Papers); 'joined-up' strategies that recognise the inter-connected nature of organisations and institutions. But, judging by the often negative reactions to the development of these frameworks and papers, and the rather mechanistic ways in which they have been implemented so far, they are still mired in the bog of instrumentalism. The emphasis still appears to be on 'capturing' knowledge and 'controlling' processes; on replicating and scaling up in order to produce a replicable uniformity that can be abstracted and simplified.

The organic metaphor highlights the dual nature of organisations, and allows us to differentiate between the formal structures that can be designed and which are characterised by institutional rules and procedures, and the informal 'communities of practice' in which the life of organisations is to be found. It points us towards the dynamic tension that always characterises the interface between them. Because of the hegemony of the mechanistic model we have paid little attention to the informal and the implicit, in mainstream development thinking.

3.4 Concluding Remarks

Communities of practice are to be found within development agencies as well as within government agencies, civil society organisations and local communities, but they have all been backgrounded by our restricted thinking about development practice. These communities of practice are informed by the cultural contexts in which they are embedded, and meanings are established and negotiated in those contexts. While certain sorts of communities of practice have been the objects of the anthropological gaze since the birth of the discipline, it is only comparatively recently that anthropologists have shifted their gaze 'upwards' to analyse organisational cultures in the West. In this they have been competing with management and organisational theorists who have arguably had a much greater impact.[10] A common focus on culture, both by anthropologists and organisational theorists makes it possible to align interests and perspectives in the pursuit of more effective strategies for engagement in the name of development.

Perhaps it is more helpful to see this dynamic tension as that between different world views and in the struggles between those who hold an 'organic' view of the world and those who retain a 'mechanistic' perspective. As discussed earlier, instrumentalists and essentialists are intent on enhancing predictability, efficiency, calculability, and control, and are concerned with gaining clarity over definitions and concepts; how the essence of processes can be abstracted and replicated; how we can learn from practice. The 'organicists' (if one can use such a term) view cultures and social organisations as emergent and the learning from practice takes on a rather different form. The following quotation, again from Johnson, gives an example from Toyota:

> What then, would a system of measurement look like that drew people perpetually closer to the 'pattern which connects'?...The question, 'How are we

---

[10] See Wright (1994), for an early review of the relations between anthropology and organisation theory.

doing?' is never answered in terms of quantities.
Suppose that you're working a spot-welding machine in a body shop, finishing a small sub-assembly that may fit underneath the fender. You know exactly where all the components come from, and you can see the person who takes the finished sub-assembly from you. You also have a clear idea of how the piece fits into the car. Everyone on the line knows immediately, from their own sense of sight, whether or not a piece of work is good enough to pass on. Nobody has to wait for an external measurement system to tell them if anything is amiss.

People inform one another not through numbers, but through stories...It took years to build the mutual understanding necessary to tell, and listen to, these stories. (Johnson 1999: 297)

Establishing the 'patterns which connect' referred to by Johnson above, implies a very different understanding of the nature of measurement and the evaluation of success. The patterns he refers to are nature's patterns and he argues for a need to understand how we might work in harmony with those patterns in order to liberate or free creative potential. As Sen (1999) has argued, development is about freedom and freedom might be interpreted, not just in terms of rights claimed, or choices made available, but in terms of more fundamental freedoms. These are the freedoms associated with allowing communities of practice to develop and transcend the formal institutional structures within which they are nourished, rather than controlling and perhaps stifling them. It means encouraging active learning systems with facilitators who play the roles of Socratic guide or Sufi sage (Ellerman 2001). It is very easy to slip into the belief that development is only about rectifying perceived deficits, whether these are seen in terms of social services or in terms of human rights. It is much more difficult to provide the space to learn and to move away from perceptions that the transmission of goods, services, and knowledge will produce desired outcomes. Our role is surely to 'liberate' the potential creativity of individuals and groups, rather than to 'capture' it in the name of increased productivity and a narrow economism.

Attempts to understand in order to control the process better are premised on a mechanistic and instrumental view of the world. They lead us into the production of more sophisticated methods to inform our surveys and analyses. The assumption is that the more we know, the easier it will be to control the processes. Yet we intuitively know that the more we think we know the less we do in fact understand, as the complexities of reality unfold. In fact the more we know the more we realise how little we do know. It is often assumed that an increased knowledge of local realities will provide us with more informed bases on which to prescribe actions and interventions.

The methods and instruments that we use are informed by the world views/metaphors that we deploy, and illustrate often implicit assumptions about relationships among and between groups. Those methods and instruments, whether they are quantitatively based (as in sophisticated household surveys, or regression analyses) or qualitatively based (as in participatory appraisals, or focus groups, or participant observation) are used by researchers and others who are informed by particular perspectives. If they bring to the research a more mechanistic or instrumental world view then the rules, protocols and regulations governing the nature of authoritative evidence will mean that they interface with local informants[11] in particular formal, stereotypical, limited and very partial ways. The information that is produced through these methods is usually taken outside the local context and deductions and reductions on the basis of its analysis are usually used to legitimise particular positions[12] and/or courses of action. The information obtained becomes disembodied, destined for library shelves – the instruments for the promotion of people or particular perspectives and biases. Let us recognise that behind every method there is a motive, either explicit or implicit, and that methods imply worldviews.

---

[11] Note that an 'informant' may also be an informer in the sense of disloyally revealing secrets.

[12] Note that you can adopt as well as occupy a particular position.

CHAPTER 4

Representing, Translating or Constructing? Reporting on HIV/AIDS Projects

Sadhvi Dar

4.1 Introduction

This chapter makes a theoretical contribution to the understanding of development practice. It is not, however, derived from development theory, but rather, seeks to understand NGO practices from a management perspective. This paper therefore makes use of relevant Organisational Theory that may help to shed light on developmental practices such as report writing and reporting systems.

I hope that the chapter will make a convincing case for applying management research to NGOs, with research aims clearly related to how developmental practice is understood, constructed and contested within the regime of development and what possible insights can be offered from outside it.

My research focuses on HIV/AIDS related NGOs. There are an estimated 42 million people living with HIV today. In 2002 alone, UNAIDS cited 5 million newly infected cases (UNAIDS/WHO 2002). The HIV/AIDS sector therefore is one that is facing major challenges. It is a health issue at the forefront of almost every country's health policy and a clear priority in the international policy making arena. The importance of understanding contextual differences and providing nuanced solutions to local crises – issues at the heart of monitoring and evaluation – have been foregrounded in the self-reflexive dynamic of current HIV/AIDS policy making.

The reader may already be critical of some of the language I am using to describe development. For example, I am categorising reporting as a significant development practice. Others may contradict me here by stating that development practice is not report writing, but 'what we do out there, in the development field'. As an organisational researcher, understanding actions as embedded in any organisational practice – no matter how mundane – is very revealing. Studying reporting for example, can help to shed light on how core development concepts (e.g. empowerment, participation, equity) are constructed within the organisation and how they are possibly disseminated within the broader developmental field. I will develop this concept of practice further, in section 4.2. The second problematic phrase I have employed is *development regime*. By using the word regime I am signalling my appreciation for a more discursive investigation of development. To understand development as a regime is to acknowledge development as a collection of practices that construct a relationship – a bind – that forces practitioners (and academics) to move within limited parameters of action and thought. The analysis and deconstruction of such binds and practices can be done through investigating the discourses employed to give life to an ideological concept. Such a concept could be 'bottom-up' or 'de-centralised' and it could be given life by presenting an *image* of a bottom-up organisation as current, ethical and facilitive. Whether a bottom-up organisation is possible or even exists are questions boycotted in a convincing presentation of the image of bottom-up. This notion can be better exemplified by a discussion of the object of this chapter: the report.

4.2 The Functions of Report Writing

Everyone writes reports in development. They are written to exchange information, to monitor progress of projects, and to help practitioners document 'best practices'. But what else do reports actually do? When we sit down to write a report, there is a compulsion to do so: we must write the report. But why is this and why do we feel we must make it a good report? In writing a report we express and construct an author identity and validate content by representing ideas and data in a particular format or style. Reporting systems indicate lines of accountability and hierarchies of power in the way reports are created, the way they surface and are exchanged within organisations and between organisations. The report is also used to legitimate actions carried out in the work place, motivating actors to construct a reality acceptable to the readership. The report is therefore a powerful discursive technology that can be utilised as a revealing artefact in researching contemporary issues related to NGO management and practice.

Reports are endemic in our culture. The need to measure, quantify, and account for our actions saturates Western culture and society, leading some theorists to describe it as an 'Audit Society' (Power 1997) or 'Audit Culture' (Strathern 2001). Audit as a practice is thereby re-defined in a much more broad sense than financial audit: it is a process that encompasses an array of measuring, monitoring and surveying processes. Such a drive towards audit as a global practice necessitates standardisation. Standardisation has repercussions however, one being a tension between what is demanded in terms of a homogenous data-set and global categories and what is needed or available at a more local level. Reporting systems blur local and contextual characteristics by focusing on shared activities and common goals. By glossing over local factors there is a danger that these will never surface within the organisation and therefore will not inform macro and senior policy making groups. This is recognised as a significant problem in management circles, especially when working towards de-centralisation and a horizontal management approach (Edwards and Hulme 1995).

Another and more fundamental problem that is discussed in relation to the diffusion of the practice of reporting is the way that it is carried out ritualistically, rather than for any rational reason or logic. Reporting becomes an end with no means, a process that is infused with symbolic value but very little utility (Meyer and Rowan [1977] 1991). These tensions are clearly illustrated in the way Northern developmental donor agencies operate in the South. Northern designed systems of reporting are incorporated in Southern practices without much questioning or hesitation. The reason for this is not that the Northern system is superior or more appropriate than other local practices, but because it is an accepted, standardised model for linking actions back to articulated ideas for development. Because these systems are inappropriate to the context, a fundamental question must be asked: how is it that a system that is difficult, esoteric and openly criticised remains the legitimated practice for evaluating projects?

4.3 Transitional Environments / Ritualised Processes

There has been an ideological transition in the development sector from purely handing out aid to aiming to facilitate sustainable development (UNDP 2001). At the same time reporting systems remain dictated by donor needs. Therefore while donors seek to move to more horizontal, de-centralised ventures in the South, reporting systems still shadow old ways of working: centralising control and maintaining vertical lines of accountability. For example, in HIV/AIDS there has been much done to empower clients to enable them to change their own behaviour. This is a vital component of many HIV/AIDS programmes today (UNAIDS/WHO 2002). These changes in managing the epidemic are represented through reports, seminars and conferences and one of the major challenges today is actually to work towards nuanced projects that empower beneficiaries. This transition in ideology has precipitated a debate within development, asking to what extent such a transition has transformed organisational identity and work practices (Escobar 1995; Edwards and Hulme 1995; Hulme and Edwards 1997; Stiles 2000; Eade and Ligteringen 2001). This change in organisational identity is vital for the re-definition of recipients of aid: from passive individuals to active agents of change. The table below illustrates this point using the paternalistic vs. facilitative distinction as a continuum on which organisations' identities and work practices are formed.

Table 4.1 Changing Organisational Identity Leading to Changing Recipient Identity

	Paternalistic		Facilitative
Organisational Identity	Paternalistic	⇒	Facilitative
Structure	Centralised Vertical Top-down	⇒	Federation/Network Horizontal Bottom-up
Practices	Donating aid Standardised reporting systems Rational casual inferences i.e. more aid = better lives	⇒	Sustaining development Flexible, looser reporting systems Non-linear logic applied i.e. capacity building, advocacy, agency
Recipient Identity	Static Passive Individual	⇒	Transformative Active Social

The four elements of organisation outlined in the table above (organisational identity, structure, practices and recipient identity) interact with one another and are in this way interdependent. Identities are both the end product and the precept from which organisational transition is worked towards. By re-defining core organisational values, organisational identity is re-framed. From such a change in ideology, practices and structures are re-addressed and through this self-critique, a new recipient identity emerges: one that is transformative, active and social. Such a transition and how it marks organisational processes has been acknowledged by many international and community-based NGOs (Edwards and Hulme 1995; Hulme and Edwards 1997; ActionAid 2003; INTRAC 2003). Changing organisational identity and values therefore becomes an important part of managing the transition towards sustainable development. It is the first step in working towards a renewed recipient identity. What is questionable however, is the extent to which structures and practices are shadowing articulated changes in core values. It is very easy to present identity as transformed. A simple re-branding strategy is often enough to convince audiences that a change is happening: you only have to present a convincing image. But whether this change has been internalised is something that is questionable, and difficult to measure. However, what is evident, is an inertia in reporting systems that limits how facilitative and socially embedded an organisation can be. After all, if organisations are still counting condoms, and recipients are still being 'approached' or 'contacted' by the organisations, then their identities remain static, passive, and individual.

Many developmental organisations have centrally driven systems of reporting that reflect old ways of working (Hulme and Edwards 1997). Organisational reports document little in terms of behaviour change, instead focusing on the organisational response to HIV/AIDS and occluding the needs and wants of the beneficiary. Although the development sector is keen to portray itself as a facilitator, it is questionable whether such an ideology has been integrated into structures and practices of NGOs. This is not through any fault or ill-judgement of NGO workers but as a consequence of certain practices that have gained legitimacy within the sector and are therefore difficult to question and overturn. Investigating how such institutionalised practices may foster the construction of identity can help shed light on which contexts conduce change and how other contexts promote ritual.

The way in which organisational identity is constructed, challenged, contested, *changed* through the practice of reporting exposes the subjective nature of producing and reproducing organisational knowledge. Knowledge in this case is to be understood in its broadest sense, encompassing jargon, vocabularies, and labels. In this way, the dissemination and assimilation of knowledge is a process bound to discourse (Foucault 1972). Political and social changes are accompanied by linguistic changes, creating a discourse that stimulates debate and opens up new choices as to how we see ourselves in relation to new knowledge. The impact of the production of knowledge on developmental practices is an area that deserves far greater attention than that which it is presently receiving.

4.4 Organising Development: Applying Organisational Theory to NGOs

My theoretical discussion will start by looking at one of the most influential organisational theories to surface in recent North American literature: new institutionalism. New institutionalism offers a valuable contribution in terms of situating organisations within wholly social environments. I will be drawing on contributions made within the literature that highlight organisations' embeddedness in society and their conformism to a socially acceptable way of doing things. Institutional theorists are very interested in conformity and how such conformity leads to a stifling of innovation and change at an organisational level, involving the emergence of ritual and tokenistic practices that reaffirm the accepted sociological or 'institutionalised' norms (Meyer and Rowan [1977] 1991). New institutionalism heavily theorises conformity, emphasising organisations as homogenous 'wholes' that replicate in form and structure. Conformity in the development field could therefore be understood as an act of replication: of reproducing parts of the organisation that are legitimated. By focusing on the salient features of this reproduction, new institutionalism does not look at how organisational identity can be fragmented: not all organisational members do what is expected of them. New institutionalism also has no theory of power. There is no understanding of how relations between organisations and employees are embedded in power. This is a great failing of the theory. To address this lacuna, I will incorporate a theoretical approach more popular in European circles: critical theory, which is primarily interested in identifying sources for fragmentation, conflict and agency within socially embedded systems of norms and values (Lounsbury 2003). Such a fusion will allow for the emergence of a richer institutional theory, capable of explaining the effects of institutionalism (rituals, inertia) and address the social constructions that prop up institutions (discourses and rhetoric). The discussion will end with an example of how these diverse approaches surface together through a discursive analysis of an NGO annual report. This, it is hoped, will illustrate how these two diverse world views can be held together in a discussion centred on the construction of identity.

4.5 Institutional Theory

As I wish to incorporate diverse organisational literatures into an integrated framework, and due to a lack of space, my discussion of institutional theory will be relatively selective and brief. I do not wish to enter into a description of the origins of institutionalism, but instead to point out how it relates to the question of reporting systems as homogenising development practices. I therefore begin with a discussion of a significant contribution from two well-known institutional theorists:

John W. Meyer and Brian Rowan who wrote a seminal paper on the significance of ritual and symbols in creating organisational culture. Originally published in 1977, Meyer and Rowan's article on the significance of myth and ceremony in organisational life illustrates how established ways of working are constructed through social processes. These social processes can be loosely defined as the way things are carried out and how the form of interactions lead individuals to accept a shared definition of social reality (Scott 1997: 496). By these ritualistic processes norms and values are reproduced throughout the organisation. It is this reproduction that defines an institution as a pattern of processes, 'that reveals a particular reproductive process' (Jepperson 1991: 145).

Relating this social phenomena to the organisational context, Meyer and Rowan explain how organisations are inextricably bound to their institutional environments. This act of re-enactment has been explicitly discussed by DiMaggio and Powell (1991) who conceptualise organisations as wholly subordinate to the institutional environments in which they exist. However, Meyer and Rowan are more flexible in their understanding. By this bind, organisations are by no means subordinate to the institutional environment. The relation between institution and organisation is a constructive one:

Organisations therefore are in part institutions themselves as well as being part of the institutionalised environment. (Meyer and Rowan [1977] 1991: 47)

This type of reproduction is done entirely for legitimation purposes. An image of an archetypical organisation is formed which is worked towards and respected by other related or connected organisations. Organisational changes therefore follow a route of conformity and promote the solidification of myths and rituals in organisational life.

As highlighted above, Meyer and Rowan point out that while organisations adapt to the environment, they also play an active role in shaping those environments. A powerful organisation can force immediate relational networks to adapt to their structures and relations. They can build roads directly into society as institutional rules, establishing themselves as archetypical organisations. The repercussion of these relational ties between organisations is that institutions and organisations alike adopt legitimating elements that are not necessarily efficient or effective. What evolves is an *organisational language*: 'collective vocabularies that suggest common purposes, goals and motivations' (ibid: 49). The role of language is even more explicitly tackled in their statement:

Affixing the right labels to activities can change them into valuable services and mobilize the commitments of internal participants and external constituents. (Meyer and Rowan [1977] 1991: 51)

From singling out the importance of a shared vocabulary, the authors go on to discuss the importance of accounting systems, monitoring and evaluation. In adopting practices that have a high ceremonial value, that is, practices reflecting the most up to date and expert opinion, organisations (NGOs in this case) can obtain funds, donations and awards with greater ease. The criterion on which organisations measure themselves is an externally defined one: one that is legitimated outside the organisation's own processes and is tied to that of the archetype. Externally driven ceremonial assessments are utilised as formats for accounts. Such processes are legitimated and goals are defined as reputable, thus internal power rises as the organisation is shown to be performing on these legitimated ceremonial rituals of measurement.

As the processes of legitimation become more important for organisations, co-ordinating and controlling activities becomes a high priority and exhaustive accounting systems are put in place. Measuring, monitoring and evaluating procedures are invested with ceremonial value as they promote the maintenance of institutional norms. In communicating reality, accounts also construct reality (Hines 1988). The ceremonial nature of accounting systems challenges assumptions of trust and that people are acting in good faith. Obligatory accounts of processes and outputs are required instead of promises or expectations. In writing reports, employees produce mini-guarantees and contracts every time they propose a new way of doing things, or when they construct best practice documents. In essence, employees are asked to express their solidarity to the organisation through this tangible contract. This could be interpreted as a lack of trust of employees by senior management or by the NGO's donors. However, this suspicion is not acknowledged openly and instead the report is promoted as an objective document, motivated by circumstances outside the control of the organisation and its management.

In summary then, Meyer and Rowan make an essential contribution to institutional theory by outlining the symbolic and therefore cultural value given to organisational processes. They also propose that conformity is not a mindless process without ends, but rather a way of securing resources and gaining reputation in a specific institutional context. Also the nature of belief systems – what they stand for, how they are accessed and how they are prevalent in a variety of social sources – is explained. Finally, a move towards rationalisation, through objectifying evaluation and monitoring procedures is discussed in relation to the creation of a shared vocabulary or jargon. The cultural or symbolic value of an organisational process (such as report writing) is deemed greater than its economic utility or effectiveness as a tool for information and feedback.

4.6 Critical Theory

I will now discuss critical theory which uses identity as a pivotal concept in explaining change, conformity and organisational processes. Identity construction is understood as a strategy employed by individuals and groups that produces and reproduces power relations. The construction of identity therefore has the potential to induce change in power relations. Creating and maintaining asymmetrical relations of power whereby distinctiveness must be emphasised is a process that is discussed by Knights and Willmott (1985). Such a process is played out in the interdependence of relations between the powerful and their subordinates (ibid: 25). This interdependence, however, is never made explicit – indeed it is occluded or denied (ibid). In stating this, the authors make the significant point that because such interdependence exists it can be addressed, contested, or even reversed. As power is relational and situated in the construction of identity, it can always be re-framed or re-constituted. Translating this to the case of developmental NGOs at a time of transition, this interdependence is explicitly addressed through a reconstruction of organisational image and, in some cases, by changing what is identified as a variable of change (i.e. empowerment instead of counting condoms). A re-branding of sorts is underway, where organisations are working on new jargon, definitions of success and legitimacy criteria.

Within this transition, two issues have been left unattended. First, how have jargon, new vocabularies and emerging identities impacted upon reporting systems? And second, are relational dynamics that determine power distributions between and within organisations being challenged by reporting systems?

Let us begin to answer these questions through a brief account of the changes that have occurred recently in the development sector. There has been a redefinition by development agencies of their core values and how they conceptualise their beneficiaries. This is a transition that is currently being driven by top international NGOs and is being discussed and worked towards by a number of NGOs in discussions with donors (INTRAC 2003). This is evident in the way advocacy groups have been heralded as important change agents within communities and NGOs alike. However, donors, while listening to criticisms about current reporting systems being vertically structured, are still requesting donor reports in standardised formats that often seek to quantify activities carried out at a project level. An account of where and how the money is being spent is the bottom-line that the majority of donors want to learn more about. Agency is a concept well debated and expressed in current development literature and discourse. However, rather than structuring action, it remains a concept, due to its complicated yet popular status. Employees can write about it and therefore legitimate their organisation's activities, but, in the practice of development the concept can often remain unchallenged. Organisational structures and practices are held constant, adhering to a

CREATIVITY AND CONSTRAINT

causal logic and pre-determined specific time frames. Change is still being driven and moulded by top-down management. After all, it is not the recipients of aid who instigated a re-labelling process, it was sanctioned by management and policy making circles within developmental organisations, albeit in reaction to critical voices in development. What the developmental critique did, was to shift the definition of success and reframe legitimating organisational activities. Managing and creating notions of success in the field by the top-players in development has undermined efforts to change organisations from within.

4.7 Organising Activity/Legitimating Identity: Analysing the Annual Report

Let us conclude this theoretical discussion with an example of an analysis of an organisational report. What makes annual reports interesting texts to study is that they form a sub-text (and an explicit text) of organisational agendas (Munro 1996). Annual reports are produced to legitimate and validate what the organisation sets out to achieve in the year and documents successes and failures, progress and stagnation. It is a tangible documentation of how the organisation wishes to be understood by the public and stakeholders. Because of this, the annual report can be apprehended as a powerful discursive tool that constructs and perpetuates an image of the organisation – it is a powerful symbol of core values and organisational identity projected to the world outside and also to the insiders, who work within the organisation.

To capture the constructive nature of the report, discourse analysis will be used to understand how identities are given form and a 'voice' in a social context, exposing their inherently social construction. This means that the analysis does not only look at text – in its narrowest sense the written word – but also seeks to analyse text in its broadest sense, one that ties discourse to the construction of social reality (Phillips and Hardy 2002).

The Organisation

This analysis looks at the organisation's[1] annual report. The organisation was set up in 1994 in New Delhi as an NGO focusing on HIV/AIDS related issues. There are 28 permanent employees and eight operational programmes. The organisation is very well known and it is probable that this fame has much to do with the controversial nature of the work in which it is involved. Not only does it work on HIV/AIDS related issues, but it is also committed to working with sexual

---

[1] The organisation's name is not given for anonymity reasons.

86

minorities and issues relating to sexuality. Given India's homophobic conservative culture and discriminatory law,[2] the organisation is a very rare and unique entity.

First Impressions

The report is a 41-page written document with no pictures or photographs. There are some breaks in the text, such as text boxes to highlight mission statements and a few tables and graphs. The report has no title page – the organisation's name makes its first appearance in the second paragraph. The first page of the report is a 'table of contents'.

There is a starkness to the report which could be due to a number of different reasons (e.g. lack of software, lack of motivation, lack of time): however, what is interesting is how this visual starkness contrasts to the ornate linguistic style of the report. Where the visual impact of the report is minimal, the text is heavy going. Sentences are crammed full of (sometimes inappropriate) adjectives and syntax is overly complicated, leaving the author's actual meaning somewhat nebulous. For example:

> The impact of AIDS does not only affect the livelihood of the infected individual, but has a domino effect on the person's social network. In effect, the impact effuses into the community disturbing strong bonds weaved into the social fabric. We can therefore no longer continue to 'otherize' the issue and deem it as someone else's problem.

One reason for this lack of clarity could be that the report has as many authors as the organisation has programmes. Each programme officer is responsible for writing an analysis of their own programme's progress and these voices are collected and edited by the Director. The level of editing is minimal however, and when reading the report the different styles and voices are quite evident. This lack of conformity actually undermines the intentions of the 'annual report', which is employed to convey some kind of shared understanding of the organisation's mission and values.

History and Context

The annual report also serves the purpose of orientating current organisational activities in the context of previous work undertaken and projected outcomes for the future. What is surprising about the organisation's report is that there is no mention of how old the organisation is, when and by whom it was set up and how

---

[2] Section 377 of the Indian Penal Code criminalises homosexual acts, making gay sex illegal.

long any of the mentioned projects have been running. More importantly, the report fails to mention in its title or its introduction, which year the report is authored (we can only guess this from which year the statistics are taken). There is therefore, an inevitable orientation around the present. This is a significant point of interest. Without any reflection or contextualisation of current processes and programmes, the organisation appears dislodged from any historical or cultural context. How the organisation's activities challenge cultural norms remains unclear. With all eyes focused on current activity, learning and strategy are ignored.

Context and Numbers

The few descriptive statistics that feature in parts of the report are also taken out of historical context. Bar charts and graphs compare the years 1999–2000 to 2000–2001. Numbers therefore lose all meaning as they fail to indicate growth of any sort, comparing only two years that do not show any significant discrepancies. Again there is a marked emphasis on the present that undermines goal-setting activities and planning: current activity is the only activity that the report accounts for. The need to legitimise organisational activities through counting, accounting and auditing supersedes any concern for the auditing practices to reflect a meaningful analysis. Statistics become a ritualised *obligatory passage* for legitimating purposes (Munro 1996).

Mission Statements

The organisational mission statement appears in the introduction, highlighted by the use of a text box. It reads:

Mission Statement

HIV/AIDS are complex issues that affect all our lives whatever the age, gender, class, caste, religion, sexuality and sexual orientation. We at the Foundation are committed to raising awareness to prevent the spread of HIV and providing support to those living with the virus and those affected by it, with sensitivity and utmost confidentiality.

One element that is highlighted by the mission statement is the client: people living with HIV/AIDS. There is also the issue of raising awareness. The mission therefore has a very socially orientated goal targeting people regardless of their 'age, class, caste, religion, sexuality and sexual orientation' – as HIV/AIDS can affect anyone. However, what is centralised by the mission statement is the organisation. Note the pivotal sentence beginning 'We at The Foundation'. What is interesting is how the report is structured according to programmes rather than target populations, echoing the dominating 'we' in the mission. *Activities* become the predominant element of the report, reinforced by the focus on the present and the obligatory use of statistics. With this very strong emphasis on organisational activities, the client is occluded in the construction of the *other*: the passive recipient of aid.

It may be useful to look at a set of statistics given in the section describing the Men who have Sex with Men (MSM) Programme as an example of how the client is objectified through prioritising activities:

Number of Kothis[3] contacted: 6,747
Number of Giryas[4] contacted: 6,105
Number of condoms distributed: 118,556
Number of pamphlets/IEC material distributed: 25,577

The clients remain passive: being 'contacted' or being the recipient of 'condoms distributed'. What the actual 'contact' between staff and client is, remains unclear and descriptions of staff activity dominate the section. The only mention of behaviour change in the client is described in a single sentence:

Estimates show that there is around 35–40% condom usage in our outreach sites as compared to around 15% at the start of the project.

A second mission statement appears in the section of the report explaining the Women's Sexual Health Programme (WSHP):

Mission Statement
The WSHP as an integral part of The Foundation is committed to training on issues of sexual health and the prevention of HIV/AIDS and STDs. The program would advocate for gender specific services and to support women on making healthy and informed choices for their lives.

Where the first statement was more orientated around facilitation ('raising awareness', 'providing support'), the second mission statement articulates a clearer goal of *empowerment* of women ('training', 'making choices'). It is in this section that the client is finally given a voice. For the first time quotations are used to give the reader direct access to the thoughts and opinions of clients. However, this embodiment of the *empowered* through the giving of 'voice' is not echoed by the supporting rhetoric in the main text of the section. The clients are *dis*empowered by the

---

[3] Category including effeminate, transvestite, or transsexual gay men.
[4] Category including super-masculine, usually bisexual men.

label of 'girls' and by the description of them as childish, frivolous and hysteric:

'Working with young girls is always delightful.'

'The girls were very surprised and were dying to tell anyone who would listen to their stories and newly acquired information.'

'...one of the girls was regaling with her mother with these facts when her mother laughed and said, "will you shut up now, you've become uncontrollable ever since you went to (the) group."'

In this way, the women targeted are constructed as pre-sexual who must be trained and taught, whereas men are constructed as sexually active who must be supplied with condoms. This distinction is evidenced also by the description of the women's health programme as dedicated to creating a 'soothing and confidence building experience', whilst in contrast the MSM programme is committed to developing 'sanctioned spaces' allowing 'men to make their behaviour safe'. Such identification constructs client identities that are reflective of wider socially embedded gender stereotypes and fails to challenge or overturn social norms that stigmatise HIV positive people and homosexuality in India.

Some Conclusions about the Report

The organisation's annual report could be shrugged off as a bad piece of documentation produced by the organisation. However, this would underestimate the report's power to serve as a value base from which programmes are designed and organisational members accent their own behaviour and assumptions about their work. Deeply embedded, almost unconscious beliefs are made visible through a discursive analysis of the text, connecting the mundane activity of giving an account to the more fundamental practice of reproducing actions and values in a ritualistic way.

The act of legitimating by writing and publishing the annual report constructs a framework. It is within such a framework that organisational members (and their clients) find themselves constructed (Willmott 1996). The report in the organisation's case is an account of how organisational values and identity surface in this commonly held framework. It is a tangible document reflecting how programmes reproduce commonly assumed gender stereotypes. It also uncovers the emphasis on activity rather than clients through its focus on the present and lack of historical orientation. This reflects a wider problem in development: one of learning from past experiences and retaining knowledge. What seems to be retained is a certain way of doing things. Moving on and facilitating sustainable development becomes an almost impossible task because so much emphasis is given to what NGOs do –

not how they do it. To be reflexive about how work is carried out requires time to learn from past failures and successes. However, time is a rare commodity in development circles where projects run according to compressed project time lines (Hulme and Edwards 1997).

By constructing specific identities, for example the construction of recipients who reflect gender stereotypes, organisational activities are legitimated as appropriate. The account of 'girls' behaving hysterically legitimises the paternalistic tone of the report in its description of activities and also justifies the lack of HIV prevention projects targeting women (e.g. no condoms being handed out to women). The report also pacifies the recipient as unknowing, uneducated, and vulnerable. To use Friedland and Alford's (1991) insights, the employees can legitimate projects aligned to stereotypical gender constructs by couching these stereotypes in a discourse of development. Contradictions between gender conceptions in each context (the Indian vs. the developmental) are used to forge a certain kind of identity of recipients that legitimates a certain kind of intervention. Thus, the image of the recipient feeds back into institutional norms and expectations, while at the same time appealing to new developmental definitions of success and legitimacy.

The true status of the report cannot be fully appreciated without a more ethnographic study of the organisation and this would be the next stage for further research. How cultural context and the experiences of the organisational members surface through discourse and how – if at all – the report is valued by the organisation members must be understood better before any firm conclusions can be made.

4.8 A Summary of Main Points and Some New Directions

The objective of this analysis and theoretical discussion is to promote a better understanding of how our day-to-day work activities have deep and lasting effects on how certain world views gain legitimacy and how we come to accept a certain identity or image of our organisation. Analysing any report can generate debate, controversy, and criticism. But this is not the only purpose of this analysis. There is no ideal way of writing a report – and I must stress this point – the better written or presented reports do not make the organisation under scrutiny any more efficient or worthy.

NGOs face a number of difficult and complicated circumstances. They are legitimated by their confrontational and challenging work, but they also seek legitimation from donors and other guiding or partnering organisations. In this tense and paradoxical context, institutional cultures, symbols and rituals can become oppressive and stifle innovation and also, courage. NGOs are only in existence because of their political nature: this aspect of NGO work is what makes their work ground-breaking. Instead of bending to the legitimated political rhetoric employed by macro-level forces, NGOs should be encouraged to be explicit in their political position in relation to the dominant discourse. Indeed this can only be done by fostering horizontal networks and partnerships that nurture relations amongst similar organisations.

But where do we start? Certainly, we should not incorporate a popular concept thoughtlessly into our own organisational rhetoric, no matter how economically beneficial it may be. Before we can seriously start to promote change within development we must acknowledge what needs changing. What type of power relations are we challenging? Do we even understand what concepts we are writing about? What is our organisational capacity and how can we work best within it? Until we can answer these questions we should not make attempts to integrate them into our practice. NGO management practices need to come under rigorous research scrutiny before they can gain legitimacy and feed back into constructing a development discourse.

PART TWO

CHAPTER 5

Measurement in Development Practice: From the Mundane to the Transformational[1]

James Taylor and Sue Soal

5.1 Introduction

The tension between product and process is at the very core of the development industry. It is a defining characteristic of the sector that shapes the practices within it. The products of development are many and varied, but the delivery of these is not the purpose of development. The purpose of development is to apply the resources (the product) through processes that transform relationships in society. The ultimate purpose of developmental interventions is always to ensure that the

---

* Both authors are at the CDRA which is an NGO based in Cape Town, South Africa, that works with people who are engaged in social transformation that impacts on marginalised communities. CDRA assists development practitioners and their organisations to create genuine, consistent and sustainable developmental practices in the field. For further information please visit www.cdra.org.za

[1] This chapter was inspired by a three-day exploration into measurement and its impact on development practice, in February 2003 in Cape Town. Fourteen development practitioners from around the world, fulfilling different functions in the development sector, participated in the process. What brought us together was a commitment to building a development practice that has the best chance of countering the societal forces that exclude, marginalise, and undermine people's ability to develop to their fullest potential.

excluded, those at the margins, gain greater access to and control over the decisions and resources that directly affect their lives.

The tension in development, then, is between the delivery of 'product' to the needy and the facilitation of a process that shifts power relations in favour of the less powerful. Through the lens of this tension, this chapter explores measurement as an essential and inescapable element of development practice. It first looks at some of the impact measurement practices have had on this tension, as experienced by practitioners. It then proposes some essential characteristics and practices required for the type of measurement that appreciates and supports the ultimate purpose of developmental interventions.

The aim of this chapter is to contribute towards building a body of developmental practice that is effective. To be effective our combined efforts have to be transformational – those relationships and structures in society that restrict human potential have to be transformed. In the process of promoting good practice we join with all those who are starting to reject measurement practices that are counter-developmental.

5.2 Measurement and its Impact on Development Practice

Increasingly measurement is being promoted as a critical tool for improving the outputs, effect and impact of physical and human resources. It is encountered at all levels of individual and organisational activity. Our individual contributions are measured in performance appraisals; the time and resources we use to do things are measured; our implementation is measured against our plans through the promotion of results-based management systems; our individual and organisational impact is assessed; our organisations are evaluated and measured against their stated objectives in order to be held accountable and to access resources to sustain ourselves. As development practitioners we are not alone in this. We are but a small part of a world that is dominated by a deep-seated adherence to what is essentially a scientific and instrumentalist way of relating in and to the world.

As development practitioners we are bound to shape the use of measurement towards meeting the needs of our purpose. We cannot allow the process of measurement to undermine it. The simple logic of measurement can best serve the interests of development practice by gauging the extent to which 'what' we bring and 'how' we bring it contributes towards the achievement of our developmental purpose. Because of the immense difficulty and complexity of what we are attempting to achieve, measurement itself must be measured in its ability to contribute towards our learning. Our purpose is too urgent and important to waste time on activities that are subversive of that.

The experience of many who have been measuring, and have been measured, gives us some idea of the extent to which measurement is achieving its developmental objective. The following paragraphs draw together conclusions reached by practitioners from all levels of the 'aid chain'.

Measurement is an Inherent Ability that We All Use

We can and do all measure. Measurement is not first and foremost a sophisticated technical skill, it is an intuitive ability. Single cell organisms can detect and measure subtle changes in their environment. Black eagles can measure when the communities of rock-rabbits they prey on are being over-exploited and are in danger of becoming unsustainable. Human beings from a very early age have an incredibly sophisticated ability to measure. Without even being conscious of doing it they can measure the amount of oxygen in their blood and innumerable other body functions. They can assess the mood of their parent and their ability to undertake a range of risky activities. Human beings can plan activities ranging from children's games, to large and complex village celebrations, to intricate manufacturing processes. Those who plan and implement activities always have the ability to measure the extent to which they have succeeded in achieving their own objectives.

People do not have to be taught to measure. Measurement is central to how they have learned. They need to be reassured that they can measure and helped to adapt and apply their ability to new situations. All individuals and organisations are in some way, planning and measuring and learning.

Measurement Facilitates Accountability

Measurement has played a significant role in establishing a more planned and organised approach to development practice. It is an integral part of planning, monitoring and evaluation. Through measurement the focus shifts from what we are doing to what we have achieved through our actions. Development agencies have had to become increasingly 'business-like'. Funds can no longer be raised without clear and logical strategic plans with clear objectives and indicators for success. Accounting for the use of funds is no longer simply a book-keeping exercise. Life without performance appraisals and impact evaluations has become unimaginable.

Learning to plan and measure our activities has improved our ability to account for ourselves. It has contributed to the efficiency of our delivery. In many instances it has made us more competitive, to the point where we win tenders from government to implement large and complex projects. However, we are nervous that these gains in our ability to measure the delivery of product can undermine our ability to focus our efforts on our ultimate purpose.

Measurement Tends Always Towards the Mundane

Within the dominant scientific paradigm, measurement reduces and standardises. In order to make sense of complex systems and processes, measurement first uses models and frameworks to reduce them to manageable segments. In the process the models and frameworks standardise what is measured. The models and frameworks are usually drawn from the reality of the measurer and not the measured. As a result, measurement is most effective and easily applied to the more material and mundane. Those things that are not easily counted are simplified and made superficial.

To the developmental practitioner measurement does not convey what is most important. It is not particularly effective in capturing value. It focuses on 'what' has been delivered and not on 'how' it was delivered; on the product and not the process; on the material not the relational; on things not on the relationships that define them; on the outer and not the inner.

Measurement then, is most efficient and effective at conveying that which is easy to count. It is the best way to hold ourselves accountable for what we have done against what we planned to do. But despite many attempts it remains inherently unsuitable as a means to appreciate that which is of greatest value to us: it cannot be used to capture impact. We end up feeding each other with information that is only indirectly related to what we consider to be really important in our work. At times it is so distantly related to anything connected to our work that it borders on deceit.

Excessive Measurement is a Symptom of a Particular Phase of Development

It is clear that some organisations have more of a need to measure than others. To those interested in observing and learning about development processes, it is clear that organisations, like any living system, develop over time. By observing many organisations over time it has been possible to detect and differentiate between different phases of development that organisations progress through. We refer to these phases as the 'Pioneer', 'Differentiated' (or Scientific) and 'Integrated' phases.[2] For the purposes of this chapter we focus on the first two, as it is our experience that measurement often becomes problematic between organisations that are in these two different phases of development.

One of the many characteristics of the different phases of development is the role that measurement plays in the life of the organisation. Measurement clearly becomes more or less important and takes on very different roles as organisations progress through the different phases of development.

Organisations often come into being as pioneer organisations. They tend to be

---

[2] See Taylor (2003).

small, flexible, low on structure and formalised procedure, high on intuitive outwardly focused practices, and driven by clarity of purpose and passion for the product or service. Because good pioneer organisations are highly efficient and their services are delivered with passion, those services become very sought after and the organisations are challenged to grow. This growth leads to the need to start differentiating tasks and roles within the organisation and developing more formalised systems, processes and procedures.

This next phase is referred to as the 'scientific' or 'differentiated' phase. During this phase, the differentiation of activities needs high levels of management, co-ordination and control. These highly measured and regulated systems have the ability to manipulate their environment and be enormously productive. But this power eventually tends to start turning inwards on itself. As measurement becomes an end in itself, it starts to stifle creativity and the ability to adapt. The crisis of getting 'stuck' in increasingly scientific processes and procedures again leads onto the next phase of integration which brings a new balance to the human and technical aspects of organisational life.

In pioneer phase, organisations' intuition, flexibility and response-ability are essential to success. Excessive measurement to a pioneer organisation is as dangerous as no measurement is to a scientific phase organisation. Excessive measurement is increasingly being recognised as a threat to productivity, creativity and even to trust, in those parts of the world where it is rampant. This fundamental principle of development not only applies to organisations, but to individuals and even to societies in different phases of development. The use of measurement is but one of many things that changes in different phases of development. One of the complicating factors in relationships between Northern and Southern organisations is that they are often at very different phases of their development. They also operate out of vastly differing societal contexts and cultures.

Measurement is Used as a Means of Centralising Control

Measurement is a very important part of our ability to adjust our behaviour in order to achieve desired results. We measure those things we want to control. Those who are being measured by others feel this very strongly. There is a major difference for an individual between being measured by someone who has power over them, and that individual measuring themselves. In the development sector there is much evidence that measurement is used to effect control. This is commonly experienced through processes such as evaluation and performance appraisal. Control is exercised simply by setting standards and benchmarks and making the judgements required for measurement. This ability to influence is further expanded through the making of recommendations, and active support for some activities mirrored by discouragement of others.

Another very common experience in the sector is that those who are more

99

powerful (those closer to the resources) pass their problems on to those further down the line. If the Northern donor 'partner' is being challenged by their back-donor to account differently for their impact, it is almost certain that the Southern 'partner' will find themselves having to change their practices in the near future.

This phenomenon is particularly rife in situations of so-called partnership. Many international agencies have ceased operational activities in developing countries and now support the activities of 'partner'[3] organisations. It is clear that many international agencies still perceive the need to extend their sphere of control beyond their relationship with their 'partner' to the relationship with the ultimate recipient of the service. Donors are not always that concerned to measure their own success and ability in building the capacity of their partners, as they are more interested in the success of the partner in delivering their services to the end user.

Measurement can Dominate and Devastate Relationships

In many so-called partnerships, measurement is experienced by the 'lesser' partner as dominating the quality and quantity of communication between the two parties. It is generally accepted that those providing the resources need to be reassured of the value of the work being done. However, measurement should be but a small part of a full appreciation of the value of developmental work. Much of the more nuanced value achieved cannot be appreciated thorough short-term long-distance measurement processes. More time needs to be spent in the kind of quality communication and relationship that facilitates real mutual understanding.

The other simple yet inescapable fact is that all too frequently, evaluations are experienced as traumatic, threatening processes that leave those evaluated feeling deeply frustrated, powerless and insecure. Very often, evaluation is experienced as a continuation of past oppressive relationships: the evaluator is seen to slip into the role of coloniser as the evaluated slips into the role of the colonised. In Central Asia, for example, evaluations are nothing new. Organisations prepare themselves much as they did when they were a part of the centrally controlled Soviet Union. The process of one person evaluating another can only contribute to improved relations between the two when immense skill, sensitivity and trust prevail.

In a business where positive shifts in the nature, quality and power of relationships over time are central to its purpose, measurement needs to be used with great care. Anything that leaves 'partners' feeling less powerful is counter-productive and anti-developmental.

---

[3] The word partner is placed in inverted commas because we feel it is used, inaccurately, to describe all forms of relationship between organisations – many of which do not in any way resemble partnerships. For further discussion see 'The Poverty of Partnership' at www.cdra.org.za

Measurement can Undermine Learning and Trust

When we have a picture in our mind of what we hope to achieve before we act, there is a strong chance that the outcome of our actions will not 'measure up' exactly to the original picture. It is out of the tension created by this discrepancy that learning can occur, if it leads to self-questioning, for example: 'Why did my efforts not turn out as I had intended?'. Ideally this process of questioning and learning leads to improved future practice.

All too often, however, this simple logical process does not take place. Because of the threatening nature of the process and the consequences of measuring, it is difficult even to admit that things have not turned out as planned. When it is impossible to avoid, the discrepancy is rationalised and justified in ways that do not involve the painful process of introspection. In relationships where there is insufficient trust, it is simply not safe to look for and reveal one's inner weaknesses. However, if we do not look inside ourselves for the reasons that explain why we cannot achieve what is expected, we will not be able to change and improve. There is much that encourages the externalisation of problems: it is often easier to blame something external to oneself – a person, a system, an event – but the developmental cost is heavy. By turning ourselves into victims, we fall prey to the most counter-developmental of all forces.

All too often, the learning that flows from measurement and evaluation stays at the level of information and does not evolve into changes in behaviour. Even worse, it can actually add to disempowerment.

Measurement Ignores Developmental Time Frames

When development is understood as an inherent natural process it is accepted that each system will have its own innate development clock: it develops at its own pace. Similar types of systems have similar development time frames, but each individual will progress through it differently. Through our interventions into developing systems we can, at best, contribute towards the resolution of various impasses but we can never speed up development beyond its natural pace without doing damage.

When measurement takes place outside of implementation of the project cycle it frustrates itself by becoming unrealistic. It is useful for keeping track of inputs and outputs but at the level of effect and impact it is often too impatient a tool to be helpful to developmental practitioners.

Measurement is Becoming an Imposed, Standardised, Specialist Activity

Measurement is at its most powerful when we use it as an integral part of our ongoing cycles of purposeful action. However, we constantly experience measurement as something imposed by others and carried out by specialists. Those doing the measurement tend to use a very limited array of standardised models and methods.

For the moment, the 'logical framework' with a few lesser 'SMARTs' and 'SWOTs'[4] dominates the development landscape. The problem lies not in the quality of these little models, but in their slavish application in all situations. This undifferentiated use of tools and techniques is non-developmental.

Our own measurement, following our own designs never appears to suffice. We are all forced to report endlessly, but these reports never seem to be enough for those who demand them. Enormous amounts of money are being spent on specialist evaluations that are occasionally good enough to state what those involved in the project or programme already knew.

If measurement is to become a part of our own learning, we must own and control the process.

5.3 Towards Developmental Measurement

Presently, the way measurement is being applied is most successful at enabling organisations and individuals to hold others accountable. Whilst it is experienced as a powerful and formative force in relationships, its impact is not helping to shift power relations in favour of the less powerful. In this section, we start exploring what developmental measurement might look and feel like. First, we look at what developmental measurement must achieve. We suggest a few criteria for developmental measurement that could be used for measuring measurement itself. These criteria will help us assess whether measurement is serving our developmental purpose. Finally, we share some characteristic elements of developmental measurement practice. Here we look more at how it should be done rather than presenting the detail of standardised tools and techniques, since there are more of these available than practitioners have the skill to use appropriately. As such, we will consider some basic principles of practice that should guide the practitioner in building their practice and 'toolbox'.

Measurement Must First do What it is Good at, Quickly and Simply

Measurement works best at the more mundane material level: at measuring inputs and outputs. On occasion it is also helpful at the level of effect or outcomes. These basic levels are absolutely vital for development practice, and form its foundation. After all, development does occur through the delivery of products and services and development organisations must be able to deliver their services properly, and account for what they have done. If they cannot do this they should not receive resources to continue functioning, since inability to master basic activity suggests

---

[4] These acronyms refer to methods used to assess design of objectives and strategic management, respectively.

little probability that they will be effective in the more complex developmental aspect of their practice.

Equally, if those providing the resources cannot articulate clearly and simply what the basic minimum 'non-negotiable' accountability requirements are, they are not fit to be stewards of development resources. The more technical 'accounting' type measurement at this level should simply be done - and done as simply as possible. Appropriate methods should be sought to ensure that it is not a difficult task. All too often it is made difficult by over complicated standardised and bureaucratic systems and procedures.

Planning, monitoring and evaluation at this level has made a very important contribution to the sector, but it is only the beginning. Those making resources available to anyone at any level in the chain must make this a condition. The developmental aspect of this part of measurement is to help 'partners' understand how easy it is, by assisting them to find ways that are appropriate for them. What often confuses and confounds is the common practice of imposing systems that are more suited to the provider of the resources.

Developmental Measurement is Transformational

Developmental practitioners who are committed to going beyond the delivery of product must find ways of using measurement to inform and build their practice. After the relatively simple measurement of product, it must concentrate on purpose and process. Its focus must always be on the higher purpose of development, and as such, must avoid being drawn towards the more easily measurable levels. It must rise to the challenge of ensuring that good practice is informed by a focus on the ultimate objective: really challenging and changing the world.

The 'counting' type of measurement really begins to show the strain at this level. There are many efforts to combine the 'quantitative' with the 'qualitative'. The problem, when we move into the realm of measuring relationships, is that attribution becomes virtually impossible. One simply cannot attribute impact to input because of the complexity that results from the interconnectedness of all things. Measuring changes in relationships has as much to do with emotion as it does with rationality. It is more about ideas and actions than information and data.

The concept and convention of measuring is hindering rather than helping us appreciate the impact of our efforts at the more complex levels of social and relational impact. There have been many creative efforts to quantify quality, but they remain fixed on objects themselves, rather than what happens between them. Perhaps we need to let go of the word 'measurement' when attempting to capture shifts and movements between social entities. We should consider the word 'capture' rather than measure or appreciate (as in appreciative enquiry). We need to find a word that supports creative process rather than one that reflects a counting mentality.

Developmental measurement must contain within it the ability to apprehend and describe changes in the nature and quality of relationships over time. But in addition to this it must rise above the mundane in order to contribute towards the transformation of relationships. Successful developmental measurement focuses intentions in ways that spark creativity. It does not reduce the complexity of life in order to capture it in small boxes. It faces the challenge of working holistically.

Measurement Must Improve the Efficacy of Practice

Measurement starts with practice, and should end in improved practice. It must always begin by clarifying and understanding plans and intentions, before looking at what was done and achieved, and comparing this to what was intended. The circle must then be completed: the learning that is derived as a result of measurement must lead to improved future practice.

Despite all the rhetoric claiming that the purpose of measurement is learning (as well as accountability) it is difficult to detect its impact. The gap between knowledge about development practice and the actual quality of what is done in the name of development is unacceptable. A cost-benefit analysis of evaluations in the sector and their impact on improved practice would make us reconsider the resources invested in this activity. We know that a lot of measurement activity produces information that we simply do not have the capacity or time to process and use meaningfully.

Developmental measurement must improve the quality of practice of those being measured.

Measurement Must Contribute Towards Shifting Relationships through Learning

The tendency of measurement to centralise control is directly contrary to the developmental purpose. Developmental measurement must promote consciousness, openness, honesty and depth – particularly in relationship to ourselves. It must be experienced first as contributing to ongoing learning and, second, as a means of holding oneself accountable. If it is experienced, primarily, as being for someone else, the potential to learn from the process will be minimised.

Measurement must build confidence by facing failure, celebrating success and learning from both. It must contribute towards relationships that empower, from dependency through independence towards interdependence. Above all, it must always leave the measured party with a greater degree of control, rather than less.

Developmental measurement must constantly create the tension that prompts learning – that results in change – that impacts positively on relationships. What makes transformational learning different, and much more challenging, is the fact that in order to take on new forms one first has to let go of the old.

5.4 Principles for Measurement in Developmental Practice

Developmental Measurement is Always 'From the Inside out'

Measuring someone else with the expectation that they will draw learning from the experience is in its essence instrumentalist, controlling and counter-developmental. Developmental measurement is measurement undertaken by an individual on the understanding that he or she will be the primary beneficiary of the learning.

The power in relationships starts shifting when individual parties become more conscious of, and connected to, the power that they have. It is not a 'top-down' or 'bottom-up' process. Power is not given through empowerment from the top or taken from the bottom without first finding a source of power from within. The power that transforms starts as an 'inside-out' process. When power is wrested from the top to the bottom it tends simply to re-form rather than transform the relationships.

The process of self-evaluation and measurement must begin with an analysis of our relationship with ourselves. We must accept full responsibility for our own successes and failures, and the ability to change and improve. We must always start with questions about our own purpose and practice. But to make sense of our impact on the world we need to explore and assess our relationships with others.

Developmental measurement is very different from the 'top-down' measurement of the recipient by the provider – it is circular, not linear. The principle of 'inside-out' suggests that after starting within, we proceed to review our relationships with others in all directions. Both vertical and horizontal relationships need to be included. In the process of shifting power, all relationships are important: those who have power over us; those over whom we have power; and those who share our position and interests.

At times, particularly with periodic evaluations, there might be value in engaging an outsider in order to bring a different perspective, specialist skills or facilitation ability. When this is done it is vital that the organisation being evaluated owns and controls the process. Those within the organisation must decide what the questions are that need to be asked and what the learning and accountability needs are. If outsiders are engaged to do some of the work, they must be hired, instructed, managed, monitored and paid (or not paid) by the organisation being evaluated. This arrangement increases the chance of the external service provider taking seriously the needs of the organisation being evaluated.

The information and conclusions gained through this process are then used to account for ourselves (becoming accountable), rather than being held accountable by others. This fulfils the basic requirement of shifting power to 'the measured'. The organisation providing resources already has power over the recipient. If there is any doubt about the honesty or 'objectivity' of the report they have every right to audit the organisation. But this approach is being promoted from experience of 'partnerships' where the quality of relationships is such that there is enough knowledge of each other that this 'policing' is not necessary. By spending time, energy and resources building relationships with – rather than evaluating – our partners we will know whether to trust them or not. Encouraging 'partners' to evaluate themselves contributes enormously to building relationships and trust.

What is being suggested is not that others should be excluded from evaluations but that when an organisation is involved in commissioning an evaluation it is understood that that organisation and its members are the primary learner expected to benefit from the process. The less powerful 'partner' is usually more than willing to be the subject of the evaluation if they know that the success and practice being measured and judged is not their own. What is then being measured is the more powerful 'partner's' impact on those they serve – on the quality of their services.

If organisations supporting others are concerned about their 'partner's' ability to measure and evaluate themselves they must not under any circumstances take over the task. Their developmental responsibility is to convince the organisation that they have the ability to do it themselves. They must facilitate processes that connect their 'partners' to their own innate knowledge of measurement. This must then be built upon until they can design a process that is appropriate to their own skills, phase of development, and needs.

If we all evaluate ourselves honestly and share our findings with each other we will be contributing to the building of a development sector that is worthy of its name, and to a real chance of achieving its purpose. We must have the courage to challenge those who are not honest and hold them accountable for their dishonesty when it is a threat to our purpose.

Developmental Measurement is not an Event but an Orientation

If developmental measurement comes from the inside out, then it is not something that can be occasionally forced on individuals by those with greater influence. Measurement is but one part of a self-consciousness orientation. It is a part of an orientation based on a belief that by acting with intent and a commitment to ongoing learning one can shape one's world, and not end up a victim. It stems from taking pride in what one does and responsibility for the effect it has on others. It is based on a self-critical questioning approach to life.

Measurement should be built into all formal aspects of our work including planning, monitoring and evaluation. But also in the less formal pondering, wondering, and questioning that turns a job into a challenging life task.

Developmental Measurement Builds from the Parts to the Whole

Scientific measurement reduces things to the point where they can be counted. The value of its contribution stems from the fact that it is reductionist. It simplifies and standardises. The logical framework approach to planning and measurement is a good example of this. It is designed to reduce the enormously complex social process to the point where it can fit into a series of boxes, and be measured using SMART objectives and OVIs (objectively verifiable indicators). The point has already been made that these tools are effective at the level of input/output but decreasingly so for impact.

To really appreciate or capture the changes that are of most importance to developmental practitioners we cannot reduce things of quality to quantities and little boxes. We cannot only consider the part of what is important to us that is most easily measured – we need to be working with the whole. This is a very practical dilemma that faces all those responsible for reporting on their progress and achievements. Those closest to the actual 'coalface' of development practice are overwhelmed by the quantity of qualitative information they have. It is impossible for them to convey it to others without reducing its volume. They do not have the time to collate it all, and even if they did, it would be useless to those who need it.

But to the developmental practitioner the issue of quantity is secondary. The real concern is with quality. The potential learning for improved practice that can be drawn from the charts, graphs and tables of reduced information is very limited. Our challenge is to appreciate the whole – and this requires a completely different orientation and approach to that of the reductionist, rational and scientific. Developmental practice needs to draw as much from the creative arts as it does from science, it needs to draw on the intuitive 'right side of the brain', as much as the rational.

When working with highly complex social systems it is not possible to engage with and make sense of the whole. In order to start gathering information on which to base some understanding we have to use models that give us a way in to the system. These models assist in gathering, capturing and interrogating information that is meaningful. It helps us take the system apart, and understand the parts, their function, and even something about how they relate to each other. But it is limited in its ability to help us understand the real meaning of the whole.

Taking one human individual as an example of a social system, we can clarify the point. There are many models that help us make sense of the human being. Medical models help us understand the organs, their functions and relationships to each other. There are psychological models that help us gain insight into the workings of the mind. There are models that further differentiate between the body, mind, spirit, and soul. There are methods to assist us in looking at how people have been shaped through their social interactions and relationships. Even if we were to apply all of these, we would not yet have a means of conveying the essence of the person. This is the challenge of holism – to capture the essence of the whole. The underlying principle is that the whole is always more than the sum of its parts.

The ability to capture and communicate the essence, or essential character, of complex systems and the relationships between them must be a core competence of the truly developmental practitioner. This is a skill that can, and must, be learned and developed. The ability to characterise is central to all art forms, and developmental practice is as much an art as it is a science. There are practitioners already using this skill to great effect. It is providing people and organisations with insights into themselves that have more depth and meaning than other forms of measurement are capable of. There are simple and practical ways of doing this that involve creative activities like storytelling, drawing and painting, characterisation exercises, role-plays, and the use of metaphors.

Again, it takes courage to start implementing these approaches in a world dominated by scientific cynicism. There is, however, much proof that there is a side of all people that is more moved by a good story than a graph. There is no doubt that a story or a picture can capture more of the nuance and complexity of the human condition and potential than a graph ever will. Equally, numbers have the enormous power of the finite. To meet the challenges we face in development, we need to bring together the use of statistics with our creative ability to interpret the less tangible outcomes of our work.

Measurement is but a Part of Developmental Practice

However vital measurement might be, it is but a small part of development practice. Measurement is becoming a major focus in the development sector but its contribution must be kept in perspective. Ongoing measurement can play a significant role in informing and improving practice that has the best chance of contributing to developmental change. But in and of itself it has as much chance of undermining what we are trying to achieve as contributing towards it. The difficult part is achieving the shifts in relationships, not measuring them. When they happen they are all too easy to observe and appreciate.

At best, measurement is but one aspect of the reflective learning part of developmental practice. It focuses attention on practice in order to improve it. Measurement will come into its own in development practice when it addresses the dilemmas and challenges that are most central to our task: when we develop the skills to engage in measurement in ways that bring complex systems to life rather than reduce them in order to control them. In seeking to understand our impact more deeply through measurement, we must generate better questions rather than superficial answers. We must measure our practice in ways that inspire, challenge and make us more conscious, always building on the mundane towards transformation.

Measurement must be Undertaken with Courage in Search of Truth

In practice, measurement is too often undertaken with expediency and efficiency foremost in mind. Developmental measurement must not fall into the trap of supporting the pretence that development is easy and that we have the answers and ability to achieve what we are attempting. We don't! If our relationships are based on this premise, we start off with a lie, and all our communications thereafter have to perpetuate it. The most critical relationship of all is with ourselves. We have to have the courage to ask ourselves the difficult questions, to challenge ourselves, to live with the reality of how long it really takes for developmental transformations to come about. Then we have to have the courage to share this with others – particularly those who have power over us. We have to call the big development bluff.

A quantum universe is enacted only in an environment rich in relationships. Nothing happens in the quantum world without something countering something else. Nothing is independent of the relationships that occur. I am constantly creating the world – evoking it, not discovering it – as I participate in all its many interactions. This is a world of process, not a world of things.[5]

---

[5] Margaret J. Wheatley (2001) *Leadership and the New Science: Discovering Order in a Chaotic World*. San Francisco: Berrett-Koehler.

CHAPTER 6

Whose Dreams? Whose Voices? – Involving Children in Project Management[1]

Yedla Padmavathi

6.1 Introduction

Save the Children UK (SCUK) is a leading international children's charity working to create a better environment for children. Our founder member, Eglantyne Jebb, founded SCUK in 1919 during the First World War. SCUK was the forerunner for the Convention on the Rights of the Child, which is the single most ratified international instrument of human rights.

The programme office in India was established in 1975. As in other countries, SCUK has been involved in emergency relief since pre-independence days. SCUK first initiated work in India, as in many other countries, as an emergency response and subsequently reacted to both natural and man-made disasters. Responding to emergencies is accepted as a mandate of SCUK in India where the organisation is recognised for its commitment to upholding the survival, development and protection rights of children during emergencies. In 1975, SCUK expanded its

---

[1] The conference keynote address and this chapter draw inspiration and information from children of project areas, partner NGOs and colleagues of South Zone office. Also, I warmly acknowledge Ms Gita Ramaswamy's and Lucy Earle's support in transcribing and editing the keynote address and this chapter.

programme to non emergency situations. SCUK has four programme Zones in India (Northwest, North Central, South Zone and West Bengal) with headquarters in New Delhi, and programmes spread over nine states. We work with diverse cultures and regions and with urban and rural, ethnic and indigenous, and minority communities.

The four strategic issues for the SCUK country programme are Children and Work, Quality and Relevant Education, HIV/AIDS and Child Protection. Disability, gender, private sector involvement, children, citizenship and governance are cross-cutting issues. The approaches to our work are determined by child rights programming, children's participation and citizenship, partnerships and coalitions, and an integrated approach. The strategic intent is stated in the India Country Strategic Paper:

> SCUK will learn from children, adapting our approaches and priorities, to support sustainable, focused and rights based programmes for the most vulnerable and marginalised children. We will add value to initiatives taken in the best interests of the child through partnerships and collaboration with different actors in the development arena including the state, civil society, children and the community. SCUK being the pioneer of children's rights will champion this cause in India and *ensure that children's voices from even the remotest areas are heard and acted upon, at various levels.*

The various levels mentioned include project interventions planned for children, SCUK itself, and State and national policies.

6.2 Children's Participation

When I first came to work with Save the Children, I was introduced to budget setting and operational plan preparation. I was uneasy with the absence of children in the process and felt that as an organisation we should be accountable to children. They should be able to determine what we do, and their dreams and voices should be important inputs in the whole process. They should be able to determine plans, and be enabled to review and evaluate projects. In this chapter I will show how it is that we have tried to incorporate children into planning, decision-making processes and monitoring at all levels of our programme in South India.

My work involving children in project management has been strongly influenced by my earlier involvement with Mahila Samakhya – the women's empowerment programme of the Government of India. Working in eight states, the programme has evolved according to local cultural and social needs. The local women's movement and understanding of empowerment has been a primary influence in informing the strategies of the State Societies.[2] Empowerment of women is seen as a critical precondition for their participation in the education process. Mahila Samakhya tries to create an environment for women to learn at their own pace, set their own priorities and seek knowledge and information to make strategic decisions to change their lives.

My colleagues and I felt that this participatory process approach was appropriate for our work in SCUK. We felt that we should begin working, and then think about how to start operationalising our plans. However, we do have three non-negotiables in our work: accountability to children, to parents and to partners. We need to be transparent and open up our books so that our constituents can come and examine whether we are working towards their dreams or not. So our office is an open-door office; our books are open for anybody to come and check whether we are spending the money well or not. We also have to achieve Save the Children goals devised elsewhere, and children, parents and partners have to understand why these goals have been set. As such we always share the programmatic vision, and discuss the changing macro-environment policies and the implications for the poor with our partners and communities.

We also facilitate the identification of immediate needs and concerns of the local community. Child rights programming and child participation are fundamental to Save the Children's approach to work. In SCUK the goal of child rights programming is to create an environment around the child which fully respects his/her human rights. Child rights violations are to be addressed, and we have systems and mechanisms at all levels which empower the holder of rights, and also hold office bearers accountable. Thus child participation is promoted in all aspects of our work.

While within SCUK we need to compartmentalise our work for the sake of financial systems and procedures, children and women in the villages do not compartmentalise their problems into brackets of education, child labour, HIV or poverty. At any given time, a family might be suffering from all of these problems. When submitting a proposal to the Delhi office, a specific code must be used, for education for example. When funding is received, progress must be reported against this code. However, whilst staff must have codes for the sake of auditing, children in villages will not understand these codes, nor necessarily see the need to divide up problems into different categories. As such, we use an integrated approach when asking children about progress.

Children's perceptions and demands have a strong influence on the way we plan and carry out our work, as is shown in the following example. Disability, gender, private sector involvement, children's citizenship and governance are all

---

[2] State Societies are autonomous programme offices, responsible for implementation and management of the Mahila Samakhya Programme in all eight states.

cross-cutting issues. During a review of our Country Strategy Paper (CSP) in September 2002, a group of 14 differently abled children demanded to know why there was no mention of disability in the paper, saying, 'We can't see any disability mentioned, so why are we here?'. There was just one phrase in the second to last page which said, 'The cross-cutting issue is disability'. Children were aghast and asked, 'How can you be excluding such a big group of children in villages?'. They became very agitated, since 12 per cent of children in villages are differently abled, due to malnutrition, lack of proper health services, and consanguineous marriages.

As a consequence, we decided that disability would be one of our major interventions in the South Zone; we would work with our partners to ensure that all our interventions addressed the issue of disability – whether it was an education project or a citizenship and governance project. Education needs to address differently abled children just as citizenship and governance projects must address the issue of recognition of differently abled children as citizens, and to work for their rights.

6.3 Monitoring and Evaluation Involving Children

Children's participation in monitoring and evaluation is a valuable tool to strengthen our accountability to the primary stakeholder further. Children, along with communities, are involved in all decision-making and project planning processes. As this process increases their analysis and understanding of their rights, so it improves their bargaining and negotiating skills and helps to transform power relationships between communities and children. It also demonstrates and brings visibility to children's competencies, knowledge and skills that contribute to village development, as well as facilitating spaces for children to participate in decision-making meetings at all levels.

There are, however, a number of risks involved when working on children's participation and child rights programming. I would like to begin by identifying these risks, since they do determine the intensity with which we work.

There are a number of factors that make it difficult to promote child participation. Not everyone is confident that children can participate legitimately in these decision-making processes. Some may feel that children do not have sufficient competency and skills. This itself determines whether children are allowed to participate in the decision-making process. It is important to do more than work with children just because a programme demands it: we need to have total confidence in children's abilities and competencies to participate. There is strong emphasis in SCUK towards participation of children in all aspects of programming, including internal governance processes. The Convention on the Rights of the Child also lays equal emphasis on children's participation rights. However, many organisations, networks, coalitions and governments working for child rights have limited their participation to events and workshops.

Also, parents, teachers and other adults can be very protective about children and they do not always support children's involvement in these processes. They are reluctant to allow children to participate in planning and review processes, as this takes them away from school, studies, families and housework. Teachers are worried that children are being taken away from learning processes; parents are also worried about their children's safety and security. One further limiting fact is children's mobility. Children are mobile because their parents travel for work. In times of drought they migrate to other states. As such we may not be able to find children who had been involved in projects six months previously because they have either migrated, been married off or been trafficked for child labour.

Other risks involve the public perception of children who have been involved in review processes and other decision-making forums. Children's participation is also often reduced to tokenism in India, generally at the level of presenting bouquets to chief guests, or waving flags at Government meetings. Some might not take their participation seriously. Also, the moment we increase the visibility of any constituent (such as vulnerable or marginalised people) they face a number of risks because of media publicity;[3] it is also likely to have negative effects on their own families and communities.

There are also problems within the review processes themselves. Some children tend to dominate: I have noticed over three years of work with Save the Children that street children face more violence from their own peer group than from adults. In any review activity, we have to be alert to deflect peer group violence. Finally, intensive participation in programming[4] also impinges on children's rights to play. These kinds of activities tend to overburden children, because they devote a lot of time to understanding the programme and its strategies and to gathering information. Many children find it tiring and taxing.

So what is the purpose of children's participation in performance management and evaluations in Save the Children? We perceive that the risks mentioned above can be minimised if children are fully aware of the programmatic interventions and expectations of the projects. In terms of monitoring and programme learning, we

---

[3] During consultations on the Right to Education, a child panellist talked about how her teachers resorted to corporal punishment and other abuses. This was carried as a lead article in the media, resulting in a witch hunt of the child. Save the Children and the partner NGO had to seek the intervention of higher officials within the education department so as to protect the child.

[4] During the Operational Plan and HIV/AIDS review, children continued with discussions and their presentation until 2 o'clock in the morning even after all adult facilitators had closed the sessions.

recognise that research, monitoring and evaluation are opportunities to learn and also to inform our own programmes and policies. In India, we have continuously strengthened these aspects of the project cycle, especially in the area of participation of children in internal governance issues.[5] We feel that our policies, our operational plans and organisational learning are enhanced by children's involvement in this process. Because of their open mindedness and their focus, children are able to bring in many more issues and dimensions, which we as adults tend to ignore. This is also important for stronger partnership with partners, children, and communities and to bring coherence to our programmatic vision. Unless and until the client is involved in the review of an operational plan, it is very difficult to have a shared programmatic vision and coherence among different partners. While setting up measurements of transparency to children and communities, most of our planning and implementation in performance measurement activities are inclusive, involving participation of local stakeholders.

So how do we develop indicators? We cannot have indicators that are developed by logframes and operational plans. Children will reject them as these respond only to organisational needs – these indicators are for our reporting requirements, and determine the organisation's ability to raise resources from external funding agencies. Instead we work with children to demystify child rights, and encourage children to identify what rights they would like to have. These are then grouped as indicators (e.g. the awareness of the community, children and parents of their rights; the commitment of duty bearers to upholding children's rights; significant changes in attitudes and practices towards girls and marginalised children; greater participation of children and duty bearers; efficient and effective delivery of basic services like education, health, water and sanitation; and the responsiveness and willingness of local governance institutions to listen to children's views and opinions).

In relation to these issues of participation, the review process measures the impact of children's involvement in planning and key internal decision-making meetings of Save the Children, as well as in communities, local institutions and administrative structures. The indicators developed looked at inclusiveness and effectiveness of children's participation, asking whether it had led to improvements in children's abilities, self-esteem, articulation, leadership skills and awareness on various issues and child rights.

---

[5] In particular, we have a practice of placing two children on the internal panel review board for job interviews. We found that applicants tend to ignore children and to patronise them. The scoring of applicants carried out by children has sometimes been detrimental to otherwise 'good' candidates. We warn candidates seriously, asking them not to ignore the children, as their views will be crucial when deciding who will join the organisation. Despite this, some adult applicants tend to downplay questions put to them by children.

We also try to evaluate – from the time children have been mobilised into sang-has[6] and collectives, up to the time of review – what kind of changes they have had in their own lives, and whether discrimination within their families and communities has decreased. We need to know whether they have been able to influence service delivery systems to be more responsive and efficient. For example, a small child was very worried that there was no school in his own village, so he made a number of visits to Block Officials. They would not listen to him: every time he went, the Education Officer would give him lectures on how children should be going to school and not to the Block Office. One day the child turned around and said, 'I have listened to you for the last four days; I have listened to you without interrupting. When I'm talking, please don't interrupt me. First, you listen to what I have to say, then you react.' In our culture, this is simply not done as children are not supposed to talk to officials in this way. He went on to tell the official, 'We do not have a school in our village. How do you expect me to go to school?'. This triggered off a change mechanism in Block Officials and the village now has a school. This is an example of how children are able to demand effective and efficient basic services, with the help of adult communities, village education communities, or Panchayat Raj local government institutions. Leadership qualities are emerging among children and parents; their self-esteem, confidence, articulation, ability to present their problems and issues to higher officials for getting redress are also increasing.

Setting Standards, Benchmarks and Dimensions of Change

Any assessment of impact is difficult without baseline data. We are addressing ten to twelve issues in every village and yet constructing a baseline requires expertise, resources and time. All these are always in short supply in any organisation like ours. Given the nature of our programmes and range of issues being addressed, baselines become complicated. As such, we looked at alternatives to baselines, since we knew that baselines would not exist for us to measure our performance against. We set standards and benchmarks by collecting case studies, profiles of children from diverse difficult situations and interviewing children about the significant changes they would like to see in their lives. Other children then reviewed fifty to a hundred case studies, seeing in them what was lacking in their own lives, and taking this as a benchmark. They also used tools such as appreciative enquiry, PLA, time-line, mapping and dreaming (thinking about where they want to be in five years' time). Not all children were able to come up with specific benchmarks or indicators, but when they said, for example, 'I would like to go to school; I want to finish schooling up to 5th standard by next year', – this became a benchmark. If a differently abled child said that 'After two years, I would like to be accepted in

---

[6] Stakeholders' collectives.

the community as a person with leadership qualities,' then this would also become our benchmark. These dreams often matched with articles from the Child Rights Convention or the Human Rights Convention. These were their aspirations and these became our benchmarks.

Based on the information collected, we began to translate our operational plans into a pictorial chart. The drawings drew inspiration from children's dreams and mind mapping exercises. Appreciative Inquiry – a management tool for elaborating organisational plans – was widely used in working out our own operational plan. The experiment with this approach enabled us to overcome major hurdles in involving children in the planning process and setting up standards and benchmarks for later reviews. Children and partners were encouraged to be provocative and freewheeling. Children's dreams were often informed by their personal profiles and on what was lacking in their lives. Based on their experiences and the violations of their rights, the indicators were grouped for performance measurement of SCUK South Zone office objectives and activities, as set out in the operational plan or country strategy paper. We then all sat together to analyse secondary data collected from MROs[7] or village panchayats.[8] We helped the children with secondary data and statistics by putting the figures into pie charts or other forms that children could understand. They themselves came up with other indicators, other standards and benchmarks with which they wanted to measure themselves.

The Review Process

The review process was the toughest part of evaluation. It took us almost three weeks to come to a common understanding with three adults working with one hundred children. The large number of children present made it particularly difficult, and the children could be tough. We needed to come to a consensus, and so had to be patient, since the children did not agree easily to everything, challenged many of our ideas and changed their minds rapidly. The selection of child reviewers was also difficult, because children have a different way from adults of selecting consultants. The reviewers themselves then had to be accountable to the children who had selected them. We spent a lot of time deciding on methodologies: there were prolonged discussions, both ethical and methodological. The different methods and tools that could be used for reviewing and assessing data had to be explained, as did the tools that could be used for interviews with different types of people. This was a complex issue, since different approaches are needed according to whom the children are interviewing: Save the Children staff, partners, other

---

[7] The Mandal Revenue Officer who administers an area comprising of roughly 20–30 villages.

[8] The panchayats are the village democracies administered by an elected body of villagers.

children and villagers. Working out indicators also took a long time, because each child has a different perception of what these should be.

Ethical Considerations

Again there were a number of dilemmas when it came to involving children in this review process – these are outlined below.

Involvement in any review process, planning process or documentation takes a great deal of time – this means children miss out on school. Therefore we always try to have the review process when school is not running, but this is not always possible. Also, there was the question as to whether children should be paid. The external consultant is paid a large sum, but it was decided not to pay the children. If they were paid, this would raise expectations in the community and there could be competition amongst parents to get their child involved in the review process. However, we try to overcome these two problems by making it an enjoyable and learning experience for the children involved.

There are dilemmas surrounding children's evaluation of partner projects. Most partners who receive support from Save the Children are working for children's needs and rights, but if the children's recommendations or findings go against them, there is a threat that they will lose project funding. As such, children might be pressurised to conform, sanitise their recommendations and be discouraged from airing free and frank opinions. As a result, there can be a conflict of interest and partners sometimes use their influence over communities to attempt to build firewalls. If a project is discontinued because of an adverse assessment made by children, then they are vulnerable to emotional and social sanction, both by the community and partners.

Finally, issues arise over child protection and safety. Inevitably, in many of the reviews we come across instances of child abuse. Whilst Save the Children has a child protection policy, this was established in London and is not culturally suitable for the Indian context. We have therefore had to demystify the child protection policy that has been laid down by headquarters and find ways of working with children that are culturally acceptable in the Indian context. Another problem is explaining to children how they must maintain confidentiality, and at the same time raise sensitive issues in their interviews. Children have a natural affinity with each other and they often share their problems. We therefore face a major ethical issue as to how to maintain confidentiality, but at the same time, address real issues.

Benefits

The benefits have been enormous for Save the Children, especially for staff. Having to answer to children and to the community has ensured that we are very careful with our procedures and accounts. We are more concerned about children's comments on our spending than internal auditors from London. The children analyse our travel expenses, and as such we make sure we do not spend more on ourselves than what children would be able to afford. The same holds good for allocation of budgets: we are always overspent on our budgets because children monitor our programme every three months and hold us to account for what we have not done.

Having involved children in reviews, we now have a critical mass of around 8000 children involved in lobbying of policy makers and ministers to meet their demands. These officials are often very uncomfortable with children. For example, during a UNICEF presentation on statistics, several children challenged a statement that Andhra Pradesh had 100 per cent safe water coverage, using their personal experience to illustrate their claims. In this way they have come to be able to challenge the authorities, and bring pressure on the Government. We find that children are very good advocates. Like many other international NGOs, we are shifting towards advocacy and we feel that our involvement of children and parents in these advocacy programmes will help us be successful.

Furthermore, children come up with provocative and innovative ideas for projects, and because we are accountable and committed to them, we must try to implement these. Sometimes these ideas are wonderful. They may not look feasible initially, but when implemented, their success is far more than would have been achieved through traditional activities. The senior managers within the organisation are very happy with the work we are doing in South Zone. What they do not realise is that this success is entirely due to the innovative ideas of children. We had the courage to implement their ideas in the field. The children own the programme interventions and regard them as their own work, not as that of Save the Children. Although the process is tiring physically, energy and enthusiasm among all our staff has increased. The commitment and passion that children have gives us the energy and enthusiasm to achieve greater heights. Difficult issues like HIV/AIDS, disability and trafficking had been integrated into all our programmes because children are fearless, courageous and will not recognise phrases such as 'we cannot do this'. Most of all, children inspire, motivate and bring fun and passion to our work.

6.4 Conclusions

To conclude, it is important to remember that planning and measurement activities are not held in isolation. Planning for the next quarter follows measurement, when gaps are identified and disabling factors are given due consideration. We strategise so that these activities are participatory and lead to a sense of bonding and togetherness among communities, children and our team.

In 2002, our boldness in involving children in all aspects of our programmes increased our learning and brought innovation to our work. It also improved team spirit and the quality of our work. Our administrative and support staff are involved and they too have become upholders of child rights. Our partners are able to identify areas of exclusion and take action to make their programmes more inclusive. We intend to continue to experiment and expand on our innovative approaches, in line with our commitment to participation and transparency.

Annex 1: Methodology
Methodology Chart for Gathering Key Information

Key areas for information gathering	Methodology to gather information from children	Methodology to gather information from adults
Which children are part of clubs/Sangha? • Inclusion (gender, age, caste, disability, school, working) • Discrimination?	Circle Analysis	'+' Assessment, mapping and ranking
Committee members' roles and responsibilities • 5 active members • Ensure all children attend clubs • Regular meetings • Look after club materials • Collect membership fee	Matrix	Interviews with parents and organisers
Issues taken up by the Sangha • Which issues are discussed? Taken up? • What strategies to solve their problems? • Are Sangha capable? • Who has benefited? • What cultural activities?	Time-line on issues taken up Mind mapping Role play Case studies Profiles of families who benefited from project	Interviews
Adult/village support • How is the village encouraging the clubs/ Sanghas? • What support from parents? • How has village benefited? • – What are the linkages between child clubs/ Sangha, unions and Gram panchayat?	Web analysis 'H' Assessment and interviews	Interviews

Future plans and sustainability • What future plans? • Can children maintain clubs on their own? • Do children know each others' names? • What kind of networking?	'H' Assessment/ Dreams/Trees and fruits Mind mapping Future Scenarios Focused group discussions	Interviews/Mind mapping/ Dreams/FGD
Support for child rights and children's participation • How do adults listen to children? • What kind of support is there for children's participation from family, school, community, partners? • What methods/process? • How can it be strengthened?	Interviews (and 'H' Assessment) Observation, storytelling Video documentation Role play	Interviews
Child-friendly safe environment in any programme	Interviews (and 'H' Assessment)	Interviews

Doing away with Predetermined Indicators: Monitoring Using the Most Significant Changes Approach[1]

Peter Sigsgaard

The Review Team was seated under a tree in a Tanzanian village on the few comfortable chairs available. In front of us was a small group of male and female farmers engaged in onion growing. My organisation supported this group to raise its income. The Review Team began its work:

– How is it going?
– Thank you, we are very happy.
– What about your activity, and the onions? Do you get more income?
– Well, yes, maybe. We cultivate more land, but prices are going down and transport is going up. But it works out well. We are happy with the support.
– If you were to prove to us that it works, what would you tell us?
– (Answer from a young woman) We do not need to tell you anything. You can just use your eyes! Or you can use your ears! We do not have to tell you.
– Eyes and ears? What do you mean?
– (Young woman) Yes, I am sitting here among the men, and I speak. This never happened before, and it is all because of your support.

---

[1] This chapter is a partly altered, updated version of a previously published article, P. Sigsgaard, 'Monitoring without indicators: an ongoing testing of the MSC approach', *Evaluation Journal of Australasia, New series*, Vol. 2, No. 1, August 2002.

7.1 The Most Significant Changes Approach

This chapter documents MS's experiences of introducing a promising and above all sensible monitoring system that is especially suited for grasping social processes within the field of development co-operation. The approach elicits rich and varied information and it is well suited for uncovering the unforeseen consequences of development interventions.

Its 'inventor', Dr. Rick Davies, pioneered the Most Significant Changes methodology (MSC) in Bangladesh in 1994.[2] Since then, a number of consultants and organisations have tried out the method to varying degrees. One can find reports depicting its use in Australia, Afghanistan, Fiji, Vanuatu, Samoa, the Philippines, Ethiopia, Malawi, Mozambique, and Zambia. The British Volunteer Service Overseas is now adopting it as an important element of its official impact monitoring system for their volunteer programme.

MS is a Danish NGO working with a partnership-based programme in Africa, Asia, and Central America. Like many other organisations, MS and its partners have been trying for years to put various traditional monitoring systems in place. As is quite typical, our approach to monitoring had two main aims. It should document our activities and their effects on the lives of people: without documentation, downward and upward accountability is impossible. And it should facilitate organisational learning where we and our partners can learn from experience and adjust to new and unexpected situations. After several years of effort, we realised that the traditional systems did not serve either of the two purposes very well. Since 2001, we have therefore been trying out the radically different MSC methodology.

With MSC, you simply ask people to identify positive or negative changes observed over a period of time within a given domain of interest. The same people are asked about which change they find the most important, and why they have chosen it as the most significant. We are not asking about changes that have occurred in the individual informant's life. We are interested in his or her perception of 'objective', verifiable changes that have occurred in other people's lives. The outcome of the exercise will be a number of recorded 'stories' about change. Some of them, but not all, relate to our objectives and it is probable that our activities contributed to the change. Part of our need to document activities and their effects is thereby met. We also learn about intended or unintended effects of the

---

[2] Davies (n.d.). Rick Davies has been extremely helpful in giving advice and has greatly inspired our current attempt to put the methodology into practice. Likewise, we have drawn on the experiences of Jessica Dart, who has used the approach extensively in Australia. I also owe thanks to Jo Rowlands (VSO UK) and Ros David (ActionAid UK) for their willingness to share their experiences with me before we embarked on our own experiment.

activities through this process. We will have to face the fact that some well-meant interventions are not seen to have changed anything. We can grasp realities as people see them by systematic, collective reflection on the stories told. This reflection attaches social meaning to the outcome of our activities and our objectives. Organisational learning takes place.

A prerequisite for facilitating new insight and learning is that results of the exercise are broadly disseminated and discussed within the organisation. Thus feedback mechanisms are important. With MSC, this is achieved through assessments of the data by influential groups at different levels in the organisation. Their choices and attached motivations of 'the ultra-most significant' are communicated to all actors in the system.

In MS, these influential groups are board members at different levels. A given country programme has a Policy Advisory Board (PAB) where partners and independent nationals are in the majority. In Denmark, a board representing the members governs MS. The assessments of stories in the MS hierarchy is important, but very little organisational learning will occur if the results are not communicated back to the people who provided the information in the first place. One learns about MS's political priorities by hearing about which changes 'the system' finds important.[3]

To improve understanding, it is also mandatory that some of the more dramatic or surprising stories be *verified* by supplementary investigation. Through this, the subjective perceptions of informants can be detailed and the (social) processes leading to a given change can be mapped out.

The method uses open-ended questions, and asks for stories rather than condensed quantitative measures. Therefore, it often grasps the unforeseen consequences of what the development organisations have set in motion. In the example at the beginning of this chapter, the Review Team is clearly looking for outcomes satisfying their indicator (money), mirroring the objective of income generation. The team came to appreciate that this objective was not so important to the production group, but that gender equity had become a key focus and had been facilitated by the development intervention.[4]

---

[3] The previously published article (see note 1) provides a step-by-step guide for MS's field offices on how MS implements the MSC approach, including the assessments by the different programme committees.

[4] The 'donor' organisation (MS) had actually used gender training as an entry point to partnership with groups in the area. The case also illustrates why it is not totally correct to label MSC an 'Indicator-free Monitoring System'. It would be more appropriate to talk about a method without pre-defined indicators, which allows people to invent them themselves.

Why this Breakaway from Orthodoxy?

The principal reason for trying out an alternative monitoring system was the painful realisation that the modified logical framework system being used simply did not work. One reason for the failure was connected with resources. Even though the system was simplified, it demanded too much work from people who already had too much to do with the day-to-day implementation of the programmes. Data were not systematically recorded and very little analysis was actually done on the reports and information that were actually forwarded.

This may also have led to a vicious circle, where partners and MS field officers were not very interested in collecting all this information – sensing correctly that it might soon end up gathering dust on a shelf somewhere.[5]

Another problem resulted from the degree of difficulty of the task itself. Partners and all other people at all levels of MS demonstrated clearly that they had problems defining objectives in an operational manner. It was even more pathetic to witness how all of us – including our hired consultants – tried to construct ambitious, non-measurable, quantitatively formulated indicators that were never used. The paucity of usable knowledge gained was very apparent in a working setting, where everyone was periodically extremely busy, inventing over-subtle systems for collecting all kinds of fragmented data. We also realised that we were sharing this misery with nearly all other organisations, including the big, official donor agencies. Everybody seemed to invest a lot in following the ritual, very few could present gains from it.

MS was attracted to testing MSC because the organisation expected to save considerable time and energy by using the approach. The orthodox system had forced us to invent and agree on sophisticated, pre-constructed, quantitative indicators, which we then struggled to feed into a system that clearly lacked capacity for measuring against them.

But there are other reasons why MS felt this new approach was appropriate. It is inclusive and participatory at all levels. It does not alienate the actors and is well in line with the ideas and values guiding MS's partnership approach. Some of our central values include encouraging partners (PAB) to influence priorities and decision-making and to engage in critical dialogue and influence the MS agenda. We try to follow through on our aim to establish an equitable relationship between those placed low and high in the hierarchy. Accountability and full openness (transparency) are other central demands for serious partnership characterised by

---

[5] In her engaging book, *Putting Policy into Practice*, Dr. Esther Mebrahtu documents the same situation for a number of international NGOs working in Ethiopia. The importance attached to M&E at HQ level was not met with the same enthusiasm at field office level. Some organisations, having invented elaborate M&E systems, now realise that they are not being used. Mebrahtu (2004).

confidence and reciprocity.

The MSC approach complements MS's work in several ways. First, it is truly transparent and free from pseudo-objectivity. It demystifies monitoring and makes it understandable to all of us. The method reflects a strong epic tradition that marks many non-Western cultures and is suited for the use of information that is already available, that has come up in Partnership Review Workshops.[6] It demands that information is used at all levels with clear links between monitoring at partner or 'beneficiary' level, monitoring of country programmes, and the whole, global MS programme. Thus, the coherence of the MS partnership system is supported and reciprocity is central.

Finally, MSC serves as a worthwhile supplement to the so-called M&E system already in place.[7] This system monitors the partnerships and jointly agreed activities by combining regular, supportive visits by MS's programme officers with a multitude of written progress reports from partners and Danish development workers. Two to five day Annual Review workshops with all partners add to the routine. The system looks very coherent and well thought out regarding formats and time sequencing, but has its limitations when put into practice in the real world.

7.2 Pilot Studies

The MS programmes in Zambia and Mozambique were chosen as testing grounds for MSC, principally because they provided different cultural, historical and linguistic settings and differed in the way the partnership approach had been implemented. Ten partner organisations in each country were visited. During the pilot, we tested a number of different interviewing methods and continually elaborated and refined the wording of questions and the explanations given for the 'domains of interest.' The latter, especially, was a heavy task. The method demands much time to be invested in precise formulations, and requires the interviewer to be familiar with the concepts involved.

---

[6] According to the existing monitoring system in MS, Partnership Review Workshops are held annually with each partner. Here, stakeholders discuss the results gained so far and plan for the coming year in light of experiences gained. The review workshop is one of a few institutions in the M&E system that is producing valuable documentation and insight learning, especially for the partner organisation.

[7] The Most Significant Changes method is a tool for continuous monitoring. It is not suited for evaluations, which normally refer closely to original objectives and are conducted after activities have ended. On the other hand, data collected and insight gained through MSC can feed well into an evaluation. Monitoring and evaluation are not two completely distinct processes. See *Evaluation Journal of Australasia*, 1(2).

In Zambia, 'interviews' were often conducted in relatively large groups (15–40 people). The results of the group interviews were promising and the method often led to dramatic new knowledge and insight.[8] In Mozambique, we used an approach closer to the system that is currently being used in further trials: one or two informants are chosen by the partner representative, who also conducts the interview.

There were a number of fears within MS that the methodology would not elicit appropriate information, or would skew the responses made by informants. For example, very open questions might be too broad to elicit specific information about partnership activities and their outcomes. However, it turned out that these provided us with rich information on political and societal context. Luckily for MS, the majority of the changes observed related to some of the supported activities, but were very often seen in wider perspective than that of the input-activity-outcome project picture.

In the partner organisations, there was an understandable tendency to talk automatically about changes closely related to the organisations' interventions and aims. We therefore stated clearly at the beginning of interviews that we were interested in the changes in the lives of people in the community. We further explained that we would ask questions about the organisations' performance at the end of the interview. Even so, the method does *not*, as many had feared, encourage informants to talk only about positive changes and to present a 'rosy' picture. We asked about 'changes for better or worse' and that was sufficient to get a more varied response. It was extremely easy for the PAB members to choose the stories later that they found significant from a country programme angle.

The *overall* result was that the method worked. It provided us with added insight, especially about the importance connected to the observed changes. Furthermore, it sometimes pointed to new issues not previously considered. Very little of the information related to us could be found in reports and files already available at the MS offices. We also found that, after posing the same question over a few days to different people in different places, we became able to predict future answers with a high degree of accuracy. This is an indication that the method is reliable and that the answers objectively reflect widespread perceptions about conditions in the given social setting. We believe that others could have replicated the exercise at the time and that they would have discovered something quite similar. Participants benefited from the use of the methodology, especially from the group sessions. 'We have never talked about our work like that,' a director of a small NGO exclaimed after a staff session. Many partners expressed surprise about how easily the methodology led to important discussions and reflection among staff

---

[8] We received valuable help from MS Programme Officers. I am very grateful for the dedicated assistance rendered by Charlton Sulwe, MS Zambia, and Roberto Armando, MS Mozambique.

about their role and the wider setting they were operating in. Many organisations decided to continue using the approach as an internal monitoring tool. Group sessions were also used as an opportunity for the 'beneficiaries' to speak out. While participants were asked to speak only for five minutes about the significant changes they had seen as a result of their cooperation with partners, several spoke for much longer, and tended to give a little history as well as recounting significant changes. The presentations caused much interest and discussion amongst workshop participants and when they came to discuss what alterations could be made to the following year's planning, beneficiaries' perception of significant changes seemed to act as a good guide. Furthermore, after one particular meeting several high level partner staff members commented on how well the beneficiaries spoke and how much they knew about what the organisation was really doing in comparison to their own understanding.

The pilot study threw up a number of interesting findings about how informants reacted to the methodology. For example, field workers (extension officers) from partner organisations proved to be excellent informants. So called 'beneficiaries' directly involved in the activities also gave very relevant answers. However, officials working at office level and in higher level positions tended to give more unspecific and vague answers. Also, at the start respondents often gave their replies in a very flowery, formal and circumvent way. This was especially marked in Mozambique, which may be due to the Portuguese language itself. It may also result from a tradition of speaking very formally when reporting to officials and the like. Whilst all respondents easily identified changes, they rarely communicated them as stories. Adhering to the methodology, we asked for stories rather than short, generalised statements. Our expectations may have been coloured by a slightly stereotyped perception of African people as especially adept in storytelling (the epic culture). It may well be that objective-oriented planning and what I call logframe-terrorism have influenced many of our respondents. In one small community-based organisation, I witnessed staff taking part in a lively group discussion conducted in their own language. The discussion was, however, spiced with words like 'output' and 'indicator'. When I reminded them that the group should just agree on a story about the most significant change, they responded, 'We first want to identify outcome based on our input – then afterwards we will invent a story for you'.

There were a number of difficulties with the methodology, however. It is not always easy for a respondent to explain immediately why (s)he has chosen a given change as the most significant. Often the answer was 'because I find it most important', or 'this is what came into my mind as significant.' In this case, probing may be needed. Also, some 'domains' are more easily grasped than others. When using the method, the interviewer is often compelled to explain the exercise using locally understood concepts rather than the exact wording in the questionnaire. It was, for example, difficult to explain the domain of 'Intercultural Co-operation'. In Mozambique, it often did not ring any bells. This was a bit surprising since MS runs a personnel programme which posts Danes with the partner organisation. One declared aim is to stimulate co-operation across cultural borders. However, the Danes were rarely perceived as agents of intercultural dialogue, but seen more as professional assistants.[9] It follows from this that the method benefits from facilitation by an interviewer. Written answers to mailed questionnaires will not produce the right type of responses. Other difficulties with the methodology are outlined in the following section.

Finally, verification of stories was not undertaken in the pilot study. However, many of the stories were of a nature that immediately called for further investigation.[10] The curiosity of MS's programme officers was awakened, and we expected that a follow up would be done. As can be seen below, this expectation was a bit optimistic. We also found that the word verification should not be used externally for these further investigations. The concept is too much connected with 'control.'

7.3 Adapting the Methodology

The pilot exercise was promising and MS decided to continue experimentation on a larger scale. We made detailed guidelines for a uniform use of the approach for seven country field offices in Africa (see note 4). We hoped to know by the end of 2002 whether a simple version of the method would work. It did not work out as expected. The process has been delayed, not least because even the simple version was difficult to handle for some offices. I suspect that the method is basically so simple and unlike the traditional approaches, that our staff find it highly suspect. Internal scepticism has been one difficulty to overcome, and we have not yet conquered this. Some concrete demonstration of the values attached to the approach and further encouragement are still needed.

However, MS is still – more slowly – working on introducing and adapting the

---

[9] MS Mozambique currently names the Danes 'Técnicos Cooperantes'. This further stresses the professional aspects of their contribution. Ironically, when the programme started in 1982, they were labelled 'Internationalistas' or 'Solidarity Workers' – stressing their function in linking Mozambique to other parts of the world.

[10] An example: a small NGO in Zambia claimed to have reduced malnutrition among small children in their area by more than 10 per cent. This is dramatic as malnutrition is rising at the national level. A sad outcome of a possible verification may be that the conclusion is based on bad statistics. The organisation had its numbers from under-five-clinics. A guess is that mothers with malnourished children are not using the clinics as much as before.

method. We are still convinced that it will be institutionalised in the future pro-gramme. Below are some of the experiences and lessons learned so far.

We now ask informants to identify changes directly and provide us with examples illustrating these changes. The search for a 'story' is not in focus anymore. We also urge the informant to summarise and condense the 'story'. If they give too long a narrative, we pose a question that has very little relation to the nostalgic/romantic idea of African people and their supposed epic culture. For example: 'If you were to talk about this significant change to a reporter from CNN and want it to make the headline of the day, what would you say?'. The question elicits surprisingly sharp, precise answers about what the change is all about.

Group interviews were interesting and often set off a long and detailed discus-sion among people in the organisations or in the community. However, working with big groups is costly and demands a skilful facilitator. Therefore, it cannot be run by the partners themselves or on a large scale as a standard MS system. However, group interviews identifying most significant changes fit well into the annual Partnership Review Workshops that are standard in most country pro-grammes. These workshops are already organised around group work and external facilitation. One way of organising this is to divide a big group into smaller units of two to three people. The small groups are asked to identify a change that the members agree is the most significant. Later, the groups talk about their results in plenary, and the big group tries to agree on one or two changes that all the mem-bers find the most important. They then state their reasons for this assessment. It is possible to conduct such a process in less than three hours. The big advantage in using this approach during the annual Partnership Review Workshops is that it elic-its opinions and observations from people who are rarely heard, even in these workshops. I am here hinting at the people that the partners work with and for: the 'clients'.

As already mentioned, we are interested in changes within a number of speci-fied *domains*. We invested much time in delineating and explaining these domains to the informants. In spite of this, we did not always manage to convey what our focus on Intercultural Co-operation was all about. Other organisations and researchers using the method have experienced the same difficulty in getting *their* conceptualisation of reality across. A common reaction is to skip any mention of domains when posing the question. Thus, the questions will be very open-ended. When a change has been identified, it is then up to the researcher to place the answer within a domain of interest.

I believe that we should continue to explain our areas of interest to the inform-ant. An important learning dimension of the method will be lost if we refrain from doing so. Paradoxically, our difficulty in explaining to our partners what Intercultural Co-operation is, brought out the power of the MSC approach as an organisational learning tool. MS got a good opportunity to raise awareness of its fundamental aim by asking and elaborating on questions about Intercultural Co-operation. We expect that, over time, the method will help shape the partners' per-ception of this dimension of the development work. We have therefore decided to retain the questions even though they are difficult to grasp at present. A sceptical MS staff member or board member will say that influencing the perception of a respondent amounts to asking a leading question. This is true: we wish to *influence our 'object' through the measurement process*. Influencing each other is what mutual learning is all about.

Related to the discussion about domains, is the way we try to grasp the wider context within which we and our partners work. For many, the most difficult aspect of the method is that questions are detached from the specific development activ-ities that are agreed between MS and the partner. We intentionally ask about changes within a domain, but not about changes brought about by our interven-tions. A Zambian partner angrily asked: 'What good is this information gathered on the changes when they do not reflect our efforts?'. There were also examples of field and programme officers who changed the wording in the questionnaires so that informants were asked about changes related to very concrete interventions. Our overall experience is, however, that even if one asks general questions about change, a number of the changes identified can be attributed to some MS/partner endeavours. If this is not the case then the monitoring shows that we have a prob-lem. The task that remains is to explain to staff and partners involved that it is of course legitimate to ask questions directly relating to interventions (some organi-sations do use the MSC method in this way[11]). However, one risks overlooking the fact that changes identified may be insignificant in the context of the wider socie-tal picture, and their social context may be missed. Therefore, MS may want to stick to the broader approach.

Some methodological problems arose. For example, who should pose the ques-tions? Some partners grasped the idea relatively easily and could identify people with skills to manage the system and the interviewing. However, in many cases MS field or programme officers felt that they had to conduct the process – at least in the beginning. This places an additional workload on the programme officer and it may work against adoption of the system. However, the questions that we feel should be posed are those that one would expect a programme officer to explore when visiting a partner. In that sense, we are not talking about something extra. For partners as well as for programme officers, it has proven necessary to 'train' the interviewers in mini-courses (half to one day) in how to apply the method, non-directive interview techniques, and probing.

There was also the problem of analysis: the idea is that all stories collected are made accessible for all in a simple database, and that several analytical exercises

---

[11] According to Mebrahtu, SOS Sahel in Ethiopia is said to be doing this (Mebrahtu 2004).

are undertaken with the material. These analyses have still not been carried out. The stories reported are still too few in number and they have been produced under very different methodological circumstances. This is one barrier. Another relates to time and capabilities within MS. Too few people can do this analysis, and they are too busy with other tasks. Third, it has been extremely difficult to get the MS country field offices to use an 'Access' database constructed for storing MSC stories. The very simple database proved to be too complicated. This means that the data are still not accessible for everybody – which includes the partners and those who produced the information. This fundamental weakness has to be addressed if we want to maintain that the MSC approach provides the system with food for thought and insightful learning.

Related to this problem was the fact that the outcomes of the exercise were only fed back to the partners to a limited extent. It was simply forgotten in some cases. When institutionalising the system, it must be stressed that the feedback mechanism is just as important as the collection of data and upwards reporting.[12]

Some feared that the MSC methodology would demand a lot of additional investment in terms of time and manpower. This has not been a major problem. The interviews and reporting in the field can be conducted in one or two hours. Sorting and discussing the stories at country programme level can be done in two to three hours. The partners should not experience forwarding the data as an additional burden. The guidelines presuppose that the MSC data are forwarded as a substitute for one of four narrative progress reports that the partner works on during the year. However, some partners have felt it to be an additional task – they were not used to writing the narrative report as envisioned in the agreements with MS.

We had hoped that curiosity would lead staff to verify some statements of changes through further investigation. This was too optimistic. We have seen very few attempts to go beyond the immediate stories. This is probably because programme staff are too busy and in some instances may also need additional skills in order to conduct the investigations. In the future, it will be necessary to push for such verification to be done. It is an element that will bring objectivity to informants' responses and it contributes greatly to learning from the monitoring process. I believe that it will be necessary to demand a certain minimum number of cases per batch of stories to be selected for further exploration.

---

[12] Jon Kurtz takes up the issue of MSC as contributing to organisational learning in an M.Sc. thesis based on data from a CARE programme in Afghanistan. He rightly points out that the MSC in itself does not automatically provide a platform for shared learning or reflection on experiences. Even if the 'downward dialogue' is taken care of, this dialogue is not necessarily providing learning, as field staff are not always given an active role. Kurtz, J.: 'Innovating for Organizational Learning with the Most Significant Change Method', Chapter 5 in draft thesis titled *Learning Amidst Crisis*, 2003.

7.4 Preliminary Conclusions

It is my guess that the method will be adopted, and used as a monitoring system by MS. There are also indications that the work with this simple approach has demystified monitoring in general. The process of verification and the curiosity aroused by the powerful data collected, will urge the country offices as well as the partners to supplement their knowledge through use of other, maybe more refined and controlled measures.

We also already now see a change in thinking about monitoring in several of our programmes. One country programme is at present struggling with a database suited for gathering data and analysing it in a simple monitoring process. Nearly all our staff now talk about change in the same sentence as they use the word monitoring. In some country programmes, we witness a new and special effort to collect baseline data. In reports, we read more and more examples of change as told by people themselves – and we see the same tendency spreading out to the partners. We are, however, still tending to produce anecdotal evidence as opposed to more analytical evidence pointing towards probable effects of the partnership activities.

The MSC system is only partially participatory. Domains of interest are centrally decided on, and the sorting of stories according to significance is hierarchic. However, I believe that the use of and respect for peoples' own indicators will lead to participatory methodologies and 'measurement' based on negotiated indicators where all stakeholders have a say in the very planning of the development process.[13]

Some people in the MS system have voiced a concern that the MSC method is too simple and 'loose' to be accepted by our back donor, Danida, and our staff in the field. The method is not scientific enough, they say. My computer's thesaurus programme tells me that science means knowledge. I can confidently recommend the Most Significant Changes methodology as scientific.

---

[13] See Estrella et al. (2000).

CHAPTER 8

Transforming Practice in ActionAid: Experiences and Challenges in Rethinking Learning, Monitoring and Accountability Systems

Jennifer Chapman, Rosalind David and Antonella Mancini

8.1 Introduction

During the 1990s, ActionAid[1] shifted its approach from a relatively narrow concentration on operational projects in selected geographical areas to far more diverse country and regional programmes, and a greater investment in policy and advocacy work. These changes reflected the different discourses within ActionAid on the causes of poverty and the organisation's approach to poverty alleviation. These ideas were encapsulated in a bold new strategy, *Fighting poverty together*,[2] which refocused ActionAid's work from delivering services to addressing the fundamental causes of social injustice and poverty. The new strategy served to highlight the disjuncture between ActionAid's vision and the organisational systems that were supposed to facilitate organisational performance. The most obvious

---

[1] ActionAid is the third largest development agency in the UK. Its mission is to work with poor and marginalised people to eradicate poverty by overcoming the injustice and inequity that cause it.

[2] Fighting poverty together, *ActionAid strategy (1999–2005)*.

system requiring revision was that for accountability, planning and reporting.

During the 1990s, ActionAid, like many large NGOs, equated accountability and reporting systems with central control and bureaucracy. As a result, staff and local partners complained of spending too much time and effort on planning and reporting. ActionAid's internal planning and reporting systems over-emphasised upward reporting, accountability to donors and sponsors and was overly reliant on ActionAid's own interpretation of change. Large wordy reports (written in English) tended to describe project activities in great detail whilst giving less emphasis to the wider outcomes, impacts and changes perceived by the groups of people with whom ActionAid and ActionAid's partners work. Despite a huge amount of staff effort spent on reporting, the organisation knew little about the lasting changes that its work had brought about in people's lives. Things had to change.

The Accountability, Learning and Planning System (ALPS)

What ActionAid developed was, and remains, challenging. A long process of internal dialogue and discussion led to the design of a new system – ALPS, the ActionAid Accountability, Learning and Planning System.[3] ALPS is a system that recognises that social development, rights or social justice can not be planned for, managed and delivered in a linear fashion. It recognises that the principles and attitudes and the ways in which we do things are more important than plans and reports. That to carry out ActionAid's ambitious organisational strategy – *Fighting poverty together* – space needs to be created for ActionAid staff to reflect and work in a different way with their partners and poor people. Attitudes, behaviours and principles are therefore fundamental to ALPS.

Central to ALPS are five cross cutting themes:

- increasing downward accountability and transparency
- ensuring real participation
- promoting a culture of learning
- ensuring gender analysis throughout, and
- recognising and sharing power.

Nevertheless, ALPS also asks for core requirements. These, in themselves, are not new. They include:

- **Strategies** at each level (programmes, countries, functions, regions, organisation) every 3–5 years
- **Three year rolling plans** (with annual updates)
- **Annual reports** for ActionAid globally, regional programmes and divisions

---

[3] The development of ALPS has been explained by Scott-Villiers (2002).

- **Strategic reviews** in the form of external (consultant led) reviews of work at each level after 3–5 years
- **Annual participatory review and reflections** at all levels.

There were a number of new and radical elements of this revised system. The first was the introduction of the annual Participatory Review and Reflection Processes (PRRPs) involving stakeholders – particularly poor people, but also partners, donors and peers – in the analysis of what has and has not worked. The aim is to increase reflection, transparency and learning in order to improve ongoing work.

Figure 8.1 Core Elements of ALPS

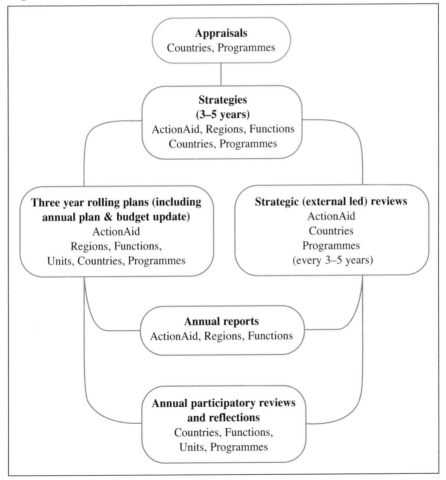

The second, more radical element was the decision not to require a formal annual report from country programmes. This is intended to allow country programmes to concentrate on the integrity of the participatory review and reflection processes.

Finally, the ALPS system broke new ground in that for the first time, it tried to synchronise the planning and budgeting processes with reviews of ActionAid's and its partners' work. It also clearly required the full backing of ActionAid's Human Resources and Organisation Development teams across the world.

Additions to the System

A number of organisational changes have occurred since the introduction of ALPS in 2000:

1. **Global Monitoring Framework:** A year after the introduction of ALPS, work began to try and enable ActionAid to systematically track progress against ActionAid's global strategy, *Fighting poverty together*. A framework setting out 'indicative outcome indicators' emerged out of work carried out by ActionAid's International Directors. This framework was piloted during 2002.
2. **Management Information System:** Second, subsequent to ALPS, ActionAid has commissioned work to develop an internal Management Information System. The aim is to identify and aggregate ActionAid information at all levels for key management decisions.
3. **Shared Learning Initiative:** ALPS and *Fighting poverty together* place great emphasis on learning, reflection and innovation. During 2002, a Shared Learning Strategy was developed to support these objectives. A key aim of this initiative is to develop systems to encourage learning and sharing within ActionAid.
4. **ActionAid Open Information Policy:** More recently, a disclosure policy has been written entitled 'ActionAid Open Information Policy'. The aim of the policy is to guide staff and the organisation on what information should be shared, and what ActionAid's stakeholders can expect or demand in terms of information from ActionAid. A key element of the policy is financial disclosure.

ALPS marked a significant change for ActionAid because it tries to set the conditions for ActionAid and its partners to involve poor and marginal groups in a real way in their own development processes. In order to achieve this, the system attempts to open up the space for community groups and partners to have greater participation in, and ownership over, programmes. It also emphasises learning from stakeholders about the value of this work and recognises different forms of literacy and communication. It encourages staff at all levels to think creatively and work in different media as well as promoting transparency, sharing and openness.

ALPS is helping the organisation move towards the active involvement of the community groups with whom they work in planning, budgeting and assessing the value of interventions.

8.2 What has Been Achieved?

In the three years since ALPS was introduced, modest but significant changes have been made. Perhaps the most important change has been the strong acceptance and internalisation of ALPS and what it stands for. Along with the ActionAid global strategy Fighting poverty together, ALPS is now seen as a key reference document throughout the organisation. It is something that staff, particularly in country programmes, aspire to achieve. Indeed, people commonly describe processes or actions as 'out of keeping' or 'in keeping' with the spirit of ALPS. ALPS – and particularly the attitudes, behaviours and principles, which it espouses – is entering the life-blood of the organisation. This has not been without effort. A huge amount of energy has gone into this internalisation process.

ALPS is creating a dynamic for change. ALPS is new, it is in a fragile state. ALPS pushes people to think. Where it has been internalised it has left staff feeling empowered. (Algresia Akwi Ogojo, ActionAid International Director for Africa 2002)

In particular PRRPs have been the catalyst for organisational changes with regards to ALPS principles, attitudes and behaviours. The picture is by no means homogenous across the world, but the vast majority of ActionAid country programmes have invested a huge amount of time and effort in the PRRPs, and feel proud of the changes these processes have engendered.

ActionAid is beginning to see changes in all of the five cross-cutting themes.

Ensuring Real Participation

A lot of effort across ActionAid has gone into ensuring the opportunities for real participation by a whole variety of different stakeholders into ALPS processes. As a result, the organisation is seeing the beginning of improved access by partners to ActionAid, in terms of understanding the organisation and being able to negotiate with it. The following example is from ActionAid Kenya:

All the Development Initiative[4] staff convened at their respective regions

---

[4] A Development Initiative is an area where ActionAid supports projects through local NGO partners and community based organisations.

141

together with representatives of NGO partners, coalitions and networks, as well as government representatives. At these one to two-day meetings, the staff shared their analyses of the Development Initiative reviews. The NGO partners also discussed the quality of support from AA Kenya, and their perspectives of the outcomes of their policy work, if any, in partnership with ActionAid. The partners analysed the relevant budget and expenditure trends for 2001. As this was their first experience in analysing the performance of AA Kenya, the partners felt very privileged, and discussed with confidence their concerns of the relationship with ActionAid. All the issues that needed action were taken on board. In one instance, the western regional management team resolved a long-standing problem involving two partner-NGOs, during the review session.[5]

Many of the participatory review and reflection processes are actively involving poor people, partners, peers and donors in new ways. Different methods and approaches have been used with different stakeholders in different contexts including participatory methodologies, facilitated group discussions, face-to-face interviews, field visits, telephone or email interviews.[6]

For example in India, it is not ActionAid who decides on the timing of planning and review processes but community members and partner organisations. This has led to a marked increase in the level of participation of the community members, particularly women, at all review meetings. ActionAid India also state that the quality of review has improved due to greater community participation. Here most review teams are comprised of two to three representatives from the community, two to three project staff and at least two ActionAid India staff members. However, in Burundi and Malawi external consultants or partners are used to help facilitate stakeholder reflections on ActionAid work to enable increased honesty and openness. In Ghana, a third approach was used, where facilitators from the communities were trained from the communities to lead the PRRP processes using PRA tools to ensure high participation. ActionAid Ghana was not willing to guide the process for fear of intimidating the communities and thus preventing them being objective and critical.

At all levels within the organisation, opportunities have also opened up for community, partner and donor participation in PRRPs. In India, community leaders were invited to regional forums meant for partner organisations where their participation enriched discussions by providing different perspectives on regional level work. Partners and donors were also invited to the ActionAid Trustees annual meeting to give their critical feedback on ActionAid's annual report.

---

[5] See IA Exchanges Special 2001.

[6] For more details see IA Exchanges Special: October 2002, ActionAid.

Ensuring greater participation in review processes is beginning to show results in terms of improved communication and transparency around work. But ensuring the participation is meaningful and useful remains challenging. The time demands on staff, partners and communities can be a real issue as is shown by these comments from Ethiopia:

Communities' time is raised as an issue in some of the DAs (Development Areas). The opportunity cost of time for communities when attending PRRP sessions was a big concern, especially in urban areas where people are busy with daily livelihood activities. The same is true in rural areas where participants had to walk long distances. Facilitators' time management during PRRP was another problem. Discussions extended beyond their time limit, sometimes without adequate consolidation of issues. How to conduct tight PRRP sessions is an important consideration.[7]

Discussions also require skilled facilitation to enable meaningful and focused discussions that will provide consolidated issues for feedback.

Increasing Downward Accountability and Transparency

Despite progress in involving stakeholders in review processes, ActionAid still has a long way to go to ensure that it is held to account by its stakeholders, in particular the poor people and communities with whom it works.

In most places ActionAid has moved from direct implementation of projects with poor people to increasingly working through partner organisations and focusing more on policy and advocacy issues across much wider geographical areas. Progress is beginning to be made in making ActionAid more accountable to the partners with whom it works. In some countries partners are now involved in the job description, selection and appraisal of ActionAid staff members. ActionAid India in particular has worked to ensure staff accountability:

At many places ActionAid programme staff encouraged partner organisation staff and community members to review the work of AA India programme staff and list down the expectations from them.[8]

This process sometimes raises difficult questions. Nevertheless, ActionAid is getting positive feedback for opening up in this way:

---

[7] ActionAid Ethiopia PRRP Report 2001.

[8] 'Learning from AA India's experience of ALPS' by Mohammed Asif, Programme Coordinator ActionAid India 2002 (IA Exchanges Special 2002).

Within Burundi, the fact that ActionAid allowed itself to be appraised (and criticised) by beneficiaries and partners at all levels in itself continues to be admired as a rare occurrence. It demonstrated for many the value of transparency and openness. Comments made by a donor during ActionAid Burundi's PRRP.[9]

Nevertheless, when working through partners, downwards accountability to poor people and communities can mean making additional demands on partners. In some cases ActionAid's motivation for this has been mistrusted as the following quote shows:

Initially, when we accepted PRRP based on the ALPS principles many of the NGO partners showed resistance towards this mode of review involving the community. They perceived it as a form of policing/inspecting by ActionAid India. Some of the partners even went to the extent of accusing AAI of not having trust in their (NGO partner's) report and hence involving the community in the review process. However, in due course the partners have understood the real reasons and see the potential of the PRRPs as an enabling tool. They feel that it has helped them better understand the issues of the partner community and to assess them against the strategic objectives. This has improved the confidence level and strengthened the people-centred approach in their work.[10]

The actual process through which accountability can be achieved also remains challenging. It is relatively easy to ensure that poor people, women and socially marginalised communities are represented in reflection and review sessions. However, if these groups are not represented by a strong community organisation then it is unlikely that active feedback to community members not present at the meeting, and future follow up, will happen.

Despite financial transparency being particularly challenging, a number of countries are also working to increase downwards, financial accountability and transparency. This has been facilitated by greater involvement of finance staff in review processes. In Kenya, development initiative reviews have included community-based organisations (CBOs), local NGOs, provincial administration, elected local government counsellors, and Government officials from various departments, especially education and health ministries. At these meetings ActionAid

---

[9] See IA Exchanges Special 2002.

[10] 'Learning from AA India's experience of ALPS' by Mohammed Asif, Programme Co-ordinator ActionAid India 2002 (IA Exchanges Special 2002).

staff have presented reports on financial plans and budgets showing the actual expenditure on different sectors at the end of the year. Participants are then able to ask questions of ActionAid staff and assess the progress made by ActionAid in implementing the plans for that year. Subsequently, the management of each CBO facilitated a similar process with their respective members, to assess the progress they had made in implementing their planned activities and teasing out lessons from their performance.

In some cases this has resulted in partner CBOs challenging ActionAid to be more frugal in its use of resources. For example in one area in Kenya it was asked why training sessions were held in large hotels outside the local area. Consequently, training is now mostly carried out locally. Similarly, during discussions on the capacity-building cost, some participants recommended that exposure visits should involve a small team. In another instance, open financial discussions led to ActionAid modifying its policy of contracting firms to implement water projects so as to include community representatives in the selection process. Similar exercises have been undertaken in Haiti:

> Pie charts presenting cost structures within each micro region, as well as the consolidated cost structures of Haiti/Dominican Republic programme (central & partner costs) were displayed, generating intense discussions and debate. This exercise was meant to demonstrate our commitment to transparency and encourage partners to look critically at how resources are allocated. It became obvious from the analysis presented that staff costs proportions were considerably high. It was agreed that AA Haiti/DR and partners would try to agree on a set of basic performance targets in an effort to increase efficiency and effectiveness.[11]

Recognising and Sharing Power

ActionAid is a large international NGO which is changing constantly, has huge power *vis-à-vis* many of its partners and which (in places) has a very dominant hierarchy. In addition, many partners rely on the organisation as a donor. As such, there is an inherent contradiction when ActionAid tries to open up space for honest feedback and criticism.

These dynamics have to be recognised and tackled if ActionAid is going to do more than pay lip service to participation and downwards accountability. ActionAid needs to do proactive work to create an environment where its partners are confident enough to criticise the organisation honestly. Otherwise, there is a danger that partners will just reflect back what they think ActionAid wants to hear. One positive sign is that front line staff are very aware and concerned about this possible dynamic:

---

[11] 'Experiences from Haiti/DR PRRP' 2001.

I have been turning this question in my mind and after looking at what has come out of our own process I feel we should be careful that we do not compile another set of old rhetoric. Our communities are smart and can assess what we want to hear and what we don't want to hear depending on the circumstance.[12]

Many country programmes are recognising this and experimenting with a variety of methods to overcome these power differentials. Nonetheless, ActionAid has been criticised for at times appearing inflexible in expecting partners and communities to follow their 'correct' definitions and understandings. It is unclear to many staff when the organisation should expect partners to learn the new ActionAid approach and when ActionAid is prepared to negotiate and discuss to reach shared perspectives.

There is also the issue of power dynamics within the organisation. Here there has been increased recognition of power nexuses and dynamics and some effort has gone into empowering staff at all levels to take responsibility and decisions relevant for their work. This is supported by the requirement in ALPS that all reports are signed off only one level up the hierarchy. ActionAid Uganda in particular has put a lot of work into organisational development processes to encourage staff to take greater responsibility.[13]

Despite the principles codified in ALPS however, the way power is used in country programmes remains largely up to the personal styles of country directors.

Promoting a Culture of Learning

When it is being used well, ALPS makes space for people's striving to learn. It offers teams the possibility to challenge themselves to improve the quality of their work. The introduction of PRRPs has led to a marked shift in the way ActionAid documents its work. Previously ActionAid programme reports concentrated on 'activities', (basically detailing ActionAid's work). Now however, there is a growing tendency for reports to be more concise and to give more emphasis to the changes our work, and our partners' work, have brought about in people's lives. The involvement of stakeholders in many review processes has led to the refocusing of analysis on what is important in people's lives.

The PRRP stands out against all other forms and techniques of impact assessment because it is organised around the community, whom the project purports

---

[12] Country Director's reflection on PRRP 2002 The Gambia.

[13] See 'The Taking of the Horizon: Lessons from ActionAid Uganda's experience of changes in development practice' by Tina Wallace and Allan Kaplan, Impact Assessment Unit, ActionAid.

to benefit. Its participatory nature results in sharing and learning by the community members, project and ActionAid India programme staff. (ActionAid India)

There is also evidence that in many ActionAid country programmes learning is having an influence on the ongoing nature of the work. In Burundi, for example, work initiatives have been revised and a new project proposal submitted to DFID in the light of learning from the PRRP.

At a global level, ActionAid is starting to see a more explicit link between the learning and insights drawn from the global PRRPs and ActionAid-wide resource allocation decisions,[14] although much more work is needed on linking work to costs.

This learning is happening largely through teams reflecting on their own work with stakeholders, but many country programmes have found it particularly useful to bring in wider experience to allow cross-learning between projects. For example in India review teams include ActionAid Project Officers from other projects. The rationale is that:

> The Project Officers are at the cutting edge of project development and administration, their exposure to other projects particular at PRRPs meant that sharing and learning between projects was ensured.[15]

In addition, the review team might include community members from a similar project in a nearby area:

> Having review team members from another development area but from the same community (i.e. tribal group) as the project partner community, ensured an objective assessment of the differences made in the lives of the community members. (Ibid.)

A significant challenge for the organisation's learning remains the need to assess the nature of its added value to partners. ActionAid has a wide range of relationships, which fall under the umbrella term of 'partnership'. Very few of the PRRPs have assessed the value of the relationship with partners, leaving ActionAid

---

[14] A paper outlining the key learning from the global PRRPs and areas needing further investment and attention was prepared for the preliminary 3-year plan discussions held by International Directors. Learning and issues are also highlighted in regional 3-year plan guidelines issued to country programmes.

[15] 'Learning from AA India's experience of ALPS' by Mohammed Asif, Programme Co-ordinator ActionAid India 2002 (IA Exchanges Special 2002).

unclear about what 'added value' it brings to coalitions, networks, CBOs' work, or partners' activities.

There is uncertainty about how to report on achievements when the work is undertaken through/by partners. ActionAid Uganda is less focused on measuring its effectiveness in building strong partners, and more focused on measuring the impact on poor people – yet the direct implementation is done not by AAU but by the partners. This issue is causing concern to some staff.[16]

Ensuring Gender Analysis Throughout

Ensuring gender analysis throughout is a cross-cutting theme in ALPS. This remains one area where the organisation still has significant distance to go. ActionAid's gender policy was introduced in the same year as ALPS, but a recent Gender Review concludes that it was not adequately rolled out and there is still lack of clarity as to how the implementation of the gender policy will be monitored:

Gender tends to be treated as an add-on. Although gender is now included in almost every ActionAid document, most of it tends to read like an add-on. A good example being the references to gender in ALPS. (AA Gender Review 2003)

There has been a lot of good gender work which has both supported and been supported by ALPS spaces. A lot of this is happening at the local level and tends to get lost during amalgamation of information between levels, leading to a lack of sharing across the organisation of the good gender work we do.

In some cases, rigorous gender analysis forms the basis of campaigning work. For example in India:

The strength of the two campaigns [Ashray Adhikar Abhiyan and Right to Food] lies in the emphasis on rigorous analytical research. In this gender is a critical variable. The campaigns are based on sex-desegregated data analysis – such as context, roles, control and access over resources, impact of state policies and programmes etc. The information and insights generated through the analysis keeps informing the campaigns. (AA Gender Review 2003)

However, overall, the organisation does not yet know enough about the differential effects of its work on men and women or what gender means in terms of its work with partners.

---

[16] 'The Taking of the Horizon: Lessons from ActionAid Uganda's experience of changes in development practice' by Tina Wallace and Allan Kaplan, Impact Assessment Unit, ActionAid.

8.3 The Distance Still to Go

ALPS has been a great success in some of ActionAid's country offices, where the idea has been adapted to local needs, and where the space has been used to inter-act with partners, to learn together and to take action on what was learned. However, in other country offices the story is not so positive.

ALPS cannot be seen in isolation from other ActionAid systems and it has not necessarily led to the abandonment of older systems, nor old ways of working. Whilst some of ActionAid's systems have undergone changes over the past few years, there is still a need to identify clearly some of the practices and policies in place that are currently undermining ActionAid's change agenda. Some of the key issues are summarised in this section.

A Need for Greater Organisational Development Support

Systems, in themselves, do not create change. ALPS has the potential to create space for ActionAid staff to reflect and work in different ways with partners and communities. This can be used well or badly. To achieve change depends on the skills, attitudes and behaviours of those who use this space well and the quality of their commitment to the principles ALPS and ActionAid espouse. There is a need for greater organisational support to develop the work of ALPS. This requires a huge investment in building staff and partner capacities and reviewing ActionAid's current human resource and organisational development policies and procedures. ActionAid has not yet built up the personnel and expertise required to give such support right across its programmes.

Where intensive processes of organisational development have been undertaken (for example in Uganda) the results of this work have been transforming. However, it is true to say that across the board, ActionAid has a great amount of work to do to address the challenge of changing staff attitudes and behaviour in line with ALPS.

Indeed, as an organisation, ActionAid has not clearly articulated what it means by the principles and behaviours set out in ALPS. Nor has it articulated expected changes, or developed yardsticks by which it can 'lightly' assess progress. ActionAid still has a great deal of work to do before it can see changes in these areas.

In some cases, there has been a focus only on the review and reflection ele-ment, without any of the planning and action element. This leads to exasperation and disappointment among partners and staff who thought ALPS was going to be something new, but it turns out to be just more meetings which make no difference to the relationships or the work that is done. Doing a lot of review and reflection adds to workload, so if it does not lead to improvements in the quality of relation-ships or interventions, then it contributes to stress and disillusionment.

In other countries, enthusiasm for and a misunderstanding of the PRRPs have led to a weakening of standard monitoring systems. This links up to the points made above about the need for human resources and organisational development support over time, and clear induction processes. It is not possible just to introduce a system and expect a country programme to change. In some countries, this support has been available, but in others it has not and staff were just left to get on with it. New ActionAid staff are often just handed ALPS without any proper induction processes, which causes confusion. In some cases the desire for more explicit guidance has led country staff to resort to writing manuals for ALPS processes, which risks stultifying the system.

Finance Staff not Working Closely with Programme Staff

Within the finance system there is some evidence that the efforts to be transparent have begun to create changes in the behaviour of finance people and their relations with programmes.

However, finance staff are currently not as involved as they should be in all ALPS processes – from planning to reviewing work – and there remains a long way to go in overcoming the past deep-rooted separation between finance and programme work. This separation manifests itself in various ways: financial figures are rarely compared to programme outcomes and impact; equally important, the reviews and learning processes are not seamlessly linked to the budgeting and planning process. Where finance staff have been given the opportunity to be involved in experimenting and aligning country finance systems to ALPS processes, the results have been extremely positive. More needs to be done to encourage such innovation and highlight lessons from these experiences.

Ambiguity of Organisational Requirements

A third major issue is the contradictory incentive set up by the *Fighting poverty together* global monitoring framework. Whilst ALPS emphasises improving downward accountability and learning, the emphasis of the global framework is to understand overall organisational progress. Although, in the long run, there does not necessarily have to be a disjuncture between the two, in the short term this can set up contradictory incentives. Pressure to identify impact can impede honest reflection and learning. It also has the potential to damage relationships with partners where their contribution is not highlighted. Pressure to 'talk up' work can be heightened in countries where work is extremely difficult and progress extremely slow (or negative).[17] In any case, programme change is neither linear, nor consistent – yet the global framework itself represents linear thinking.

---

[17] ActionAid works in nine countries, which are either in – or emerging out of – conflict.

The abandonment of the old upward reporting system left ActionAid UK's London office with a dilemma of how to report on the global goals and objectives and how to report to sponsors and donors. The upwards/downwards accountability tension is still strong, but there are signs that it is being resolved by producing the Global Progress Report as a synthesis of issues, challenges and lessons drawn from PRRPs at all levels, including that of the international directors, and also drawing from other review processes.[18] During 2003, an attempt was made to collect a basic set of quantitative information through the Annual Finance reporting process.

Early work on a Management Information System (MIS) has led to the identification of further contradictions. Initial work seems to be requiring huge amounts of quantitative information, which would seem to take the organisation back to bureaucratic number crunching, rather than focusing on the bigger picture of what is working well and making significant changes in people's lives. The tension is not the amount of information required, it is more about asking the 'right' kinds of questions in the right kinds of ways – in essence getting a balance between learning, downward accountability and reporting upwards. A balance that is hard to achieve.

Need to Communicate Changes with Donors

Fourth, the issues around internal processes of monitoring against ActionAid's global strategy *Fighting poverty together* relate equally to the external pressures of reporting against donor imposed 'logical frameworks'. ActionAid still has a lot of work to do in effectively communicating with donors how it wants to monitor and assess the value of its work with partners and with its primary stakeholders – poor people. As an organisation, it needs to challenge some of the linear thinking associated with management tools and have the courage to communicate the (often slow) reality of trying to promote social change. Change is rarely linear, is not always positive and needs to be supported in appropriate ways, which recognise context and cultural specificity. Promoting social development, rights or social justice cannot be planned for, managed or delivered in a linear fashion. Attempting to do so distorts and perverts the reality on the ground and closes off appropriate responses to contextual changes. ActionAid boldly to challenge its own internal tendency to apply management-centred 'logical' and 'linear' thinking, as well as that imposed from outside. As put by Mohammed Zakaria:

Initially we tried to think linearly: input>output>outcome>impact. Gradually, we discovered that the real world is not, nor can be linear... From a linear

---

[18] 'Making a difference in a difficult world' – ActionAid Global Progress Report 2002. Available on ActionAid's website: www.actionaid.org

model we are moving towards a learning model. (Mohammed Zakaria, Impact Assessment Officer, ActionAid Bangladesh)

Protecting the Spirit of ALPS During a Period of Great Change

ActionAid is currently going through a rapid and dramatic process of change as it joins with other members of the ActionAid Alliance and country programmes to form a truly international organisation, with its headquarters based in South Africa. There is a likelihood that this newly merged organisation will want to reduce the differences between its component parts as much as possible. There is a subsequent danger that the uncertainty of transition will create a demand for some standardised practices and tangible outcomes. ALPS offers neither of these: it offers, to those who can handle it, an exciting opportunity to learn and develop with partners and the poor and to make changes that make sense in all sorts of unpredictable directions. Alternatively, it offers, to those who are having a difficult time, a set of additional requirements that add to workload and confusion, increasing expectations of partners for actions that maybe ActionAid offices cannot or will not deliver.

ALPS as a system is the legacy of only one of the organisations that will merge to become ActionAid International. It will therefore undoubtedly change in the transition to the new international organisation. What is important is that the spirit of ALPS, which captures the essence of what ActionAid believes in and is trying to achieve, survives in the new systems that emerge. This means that the organisation has to pay attention to what has been learnt during the 'rolling out' of ALPS in ActionAid. The key lesson here is that putting the system in place is nowhere near enough to achieve real change. Increased organisational development support will be required to ensure that the spirit of ALPS is not lost among all the other pressing demands for change that internationalisation will bring.

8.6 Conclusion

In conclusion, despite the modest changes brought about by ALPS, there is still work to be done. It is only three years since the introduction of ALPS to ActionAid. As an organisation, it is still learning, rethinking and reacting to its introduction. The experience and reality of work in country programmes has to modify and change the ALPS system. ActionAid is seeking ongoing feedback from within the organisation and from its major stakeholders as to how to keep ALPS processes authentic and honest. ActionAid has a huge amount of work to do in fostering a true relationship with its partners to create an environment where partners can openly and clearly articulate criticism, and share their vulnerabilities in the difficult process of promoting social change.

The ALPS principles are very brave and difficult to realise. The counterforces to change are very strong. It takes a long time to support change on a large scale, and a lot of effort, focus and will. At the same time applying this kind of willpower can create subtle changes almost immediately and it is these changes that eventually result in whole system change.

Afterword

Brian Pratt

We all agree that accountability is sacrosanct. All agencies, whether NGOs or government departments, must account for the scarce resources at their disposal. To be accountable financially is not something very complex: we merely need to prove that we spent the funds we received for the purposes for which they were approved.[1] Thereon it is a matter of collating and verifying receipts and cross-checking activities carried out against plans. And there we have basic financial accountability (Cammack 2000).

Meanwhile, the development community has joined private business and others in stressing the need for greater organisational learning. Thick tomes on organisational learning grace the shelves of CEOs and academics alike.[2] They are often cited but, one increasingly suspects, are rarely read and almost never applied. In development terms we justify organisational learning in terms of improving our performance in delivering goods, services and support to a range of 'clients' or beneficiaries. We would expect that by learning from our mistakes we would be able to avoid similar errors in the future and hence improve the efficiency and impact of our assistance. As Robert Chambers put it, we should, if we fail, at least fail forwards (Chambers 1995).

It seems, therefore, that there is general agreement that we need to provide for both basic accountability and allow for learning from experience. At the end of the day, accountability and learning are at the heart of monitoring and evaluation. Therefore, M&E should be, one assumes, a key priority for all development agencies It is perhaps unfortunate that for many years M&E, accountability and learning were all interpreted as requirements of the sponsors of development, primarily the donor community. This created a wide mistrust of M&E by almost everyone else in development, who regarded it as a threat to their work.

The 'hit and run' style of evaluation perfected over the years, where an evaluator is valued for his or her ability to make clever and usually negative remarks about the programme being reviewed, owes perhaps more to the adversarial style of the university debating chamber than any believed utility in the review process itself. By finding problems with a programme, an evaluator had proved their worth and shown that they had carried out their assignment rigorously. Ironically, at this

---

[1] Many accountants have sought to make their profession more complex with the aim of making it easier to hide fraud, avoid tax and so forth, but the principles should be simple!

[2] For example, Senge (1999).

juncture in the process, all those concerned could breathe a sigh of relief that justice had been seen to have been done.

Fortunately, this attitude has been challenged by a growing awareness that accountability and learning should also apply to the clients and not just the sponsors of development. During the 1990s many individuals and agencies experimented with ways of bringing client views into development planning, monitoring and evaluation. Many of these experiences have been recorded and reviewed. INTRAC's international conferences on the evaluation of social development provide many examples of genuine attempts to widen the number and type of individuals involved in M&E, and hence the value of the resulting reports and processes of reflection and learning.[3]

So where is the problem? In essence it lies with the structure of an industry which is inherently competitive at the level of the sponsors but, unfortunately, not at the level of the clients. On the whole, poor people still do not contribute much financially towards most development programmes and even when they do (through, for example, their labour) this is taken for granted and does not bring with it rights to a say in management. In contrast, private businesses are generally obliged to compete for clients, putting a certain degree of power into the clients' hands.

For the Fifth Evaluation Conference we posed, provocatively, the tension between top-down performance related measurement systems on the one hand, and client-based participatory systems on the other. What emerged was the tension, not between these two approaches, but between the ability of development agencies to argue the politically correct view of participation, and their inability to escape from the constraints of unwieldy systems. Such systems find few advocates, but nevertheless tend to dominate a large proportion of agencies. Great excitement accompanies localised examples of participation, but silence reigns over what actually dominates the work of agencies that are driven by a series of procedures and approaches poorly adapted from business and the military.

Why does this happen? The simple answer lies above: most development agencies are in competition for their funding. This militates against learning, against client participation and against honestly failing forwards. It is not in the interests of many agencies to actually learn, to change what they do, to permit more than marginal levels of participation, and to be honest about failure, as this is thought to undermine their competitive position.[4] The need for positive stories to present to

---

[3] See for example, Oakley (2001); Marsden, Pratt and Clayton (1998) and Marsden, Oakley and Pratt (1994).

[4] It is not at all clear that greater openness is a threat to competitive positioning in international development. Indeed there is some evidence that agencies that share their learning more honestly are at least treated as more trustworthy than those which hide behind fabricated views of the world, designed to raise funds.

the public and other donors reduces the incentive for strong monitoring and evaluation systems based on honesty and participation.

It should be added that this is not a phenomenon that is limited to small struggling NGOs. The weakness of official agency M&E illustrates that they have a similar problem. Official bi-lateral agencies are aware that most tax payers still barely understand the dynamics of development, and few civil servants welcome serious scrutiny, preferring to hide behind the ramparts of procedure and anonymity. Multilateral agencies are also now competing in a difficult market for funds. It has been said that only the World Bank is so self-confident that it can afford to be honest in its evaluation work! A sad irony indeed.

It has been noted that the 2003 meeting of the Development Assistance Committee (DAC) Working Party on Aid Evaluation[5] illustrated the convenient collusion between all concerned not to ask too many difficult questions. Presentations during proceedings melded into a indistinguishable whole with few, if any, dissenting voices. Whereas once evaluation was at least a source of new ideas and critiques of failed approaches, it has now had its teeth pulled. Rather than derive learning from evidence collated from experience, it has become less threatening to fund academic research which can be diverted away from evidence based findings.[6]

During INTRAC's Fifth Evaluation Conference, a case study by Oscar Ugarteche of high level, large-scale corruption in Peru demonstrated the myopia or collusion of several international agencies that failed to stop or raise issues about the misuse of funds on a massive scale.[7] Similar stories have been and will be told elsewhere, but the incentives in this case were not in place to question such abuse of power and money. There were incentives, however, to penalise minor accounting and other infractions. The lesson from Peru seemed to be that corruption was only possible on a large scale: stealing five hundred dollars will not work, as at this level every receipt will be checked. To be successful, you must pocket $500 million and the establishment will look the other way. The present move on the part of aid agencies towards sector-wide programmes and budgetary support makes this a serious concern for many people. The infancy of public budget scrutiny and participatory M&E of public services does not prepare us for such a move. Indeed as some of the conference participants noted, there is a lack of consistency amongst some of the larger donor agencies that preach accountability, but whose own monitoring systems are weak and neglected.

---

[5] Held in Paris in March 2003.

[6] Consider, for example, the large number of general conceptual research grants made by DFID, with the weakness of serious evaluative material from DFID and other agencies.

[7] See Diez Canseco et al. (2002).

So, whilst donors increasingly demand the use of standard approaches to accountability and learning, based on systems no one has been able to make work successfully, even after 25 years of trying, we have an aid industry moving towards funding mechanisms that will make it even easier for the corrupt to ignore clients, accountability and learning.

Meanwhile, civil society groups find that their innovation and energy is sapped by inappropriate monitoring systems that reveal very little about what actually happens in their groups and programmes. This achieves little for real accountability and even less for learning. Perhaps public sector agencies are consciously trying to turn civil society groups into pale imitations or clones of themselves through the imposition of tedious and irrelevant systems and a virulently spreading contract system.[8] If this is so, they risk eliminating all the qualities we should be valuing in civil society.

Civil society groups themselves do, however, have a responsibility to protect and defend their value base and independence. This requires more courage and commitment to their own ideas than is present in many such organisations today. Many groups have given in to the demands of donor agencies, although these donors nevertheless continue to trumpet their political correctness and supposed commitment to real participation. Those who have stood up for what they believe in and experimented with different approaches are still with us, but we need to ensure that space is protected to allow such innovation, rather than see it swamped by a deadening uniformity which satisfies neither clients nor ironically, donor agency staff who work constrained by such systems.

Is it surprising that at INTRAC's Fifth Evaluation Conference, energy was unleashed by the opportunity for people to tell the stories of the experiences, positive and negative, that actually mattered to them? Over a hundred people spent a day in groups discussing their experiences, telling stories and examining the lessons that arose from them. Should we be surprised that hardly any of them wanted to talk about the systems that actually dominate their working lives, for which few defenders came forward?

For those interested in following these debates further, the Sixth Evaluation Conference will most likely be held in 2006. Before this conference, however, and responding to international demand, it is planned that a series of regional workshops take place. It is hoped that these workshops will encourage debate of experiences, issues and concerns in regional contexts around the globe. The findings and messages from the workshops will then inform the agenda and programme for the international conference.

---

[8] The move from grant funding to the issue of competitive tenders which use standardised contracting and reporting systems has reduced independence and innovation.

Bibliography

Appadurai, A. (2004) 'The Capacity to Aspire; Culture and the terms of recognition' in Rao V. and Walton M. (eds.) *Culture and Public Action: A Cross-Disciplinary Dialogue on Development Policy.* Stanford University Press. Forthcoming.

Austin, R. (1996) *Measuring and Managing Performance in Organizations.* New York: Dorset House Publishing.

Biggs, S. and Smith, S. (2002) 'A Paradox in Project Cycle Management and the Role of Organizational Culture'. *World Development* 31: 1743–757.

Boesen, N. (2004) *Enhancing Public Sector Capacity – What Works, What Doesn't and Why?* A literature review for the OED Evaluation of World Bank Support for Capacity Building in Africa.

Brehm, V. (2001) *Promoting effective North–South partnerships.* OPS No. 35, Oxford: INTRAC.

Cammack, J. (2000) *Financial Management for Development: Accounting and Finance for the Non-Specialist in Development Organisations.* Oxford: INTRAC.

Capra, F. (2002) *The Hidden Connections: Integrating the biological, cognitive, and social dimensions of life into a science of sustainability.* New York: Doubleday.

Carlsson, J. and Wohlgemuth L. (2000) *Learning in Development Co-operation: An Introduction.* Expert Group on Development Issues. www.egdi.gov.se

Castells, M. (1996) *The Information Age, vol. 1, The Rise of the Network Society,* Oxford: Blackwell.

Chambers, R. (1995) 'The Primacy of the Personal' in Edwards and Hulme (Eds.) *Non-Governmental Organisations – Performance and Accountability: Beyond the Magic Bullet.* London: Earthscan.

Chatwin, H. (1995) *Why Do So Many Business Performance measurement Initiatives Fail to Live Up to Expectations?* Foundation for Performance Measurement.

Collins, J. and Porras, J. (1994) *Built to Last: Successful Habits of Visionary Companies.* London: Century.

Cooke, B. and Kothari, U. (2001) *Participation: The New Tyranny?* London: Zed Press.

DAC (1999) *Scoping study of donor poverty reduction policies and practices.* London: Overseas Development Institute.

Davies, R. (n.d.) ' An evolutionary approach to facilitating organisational learning: An experiment by the Christian Commission for Development in Bangladesh.' http://www.swan.ac.uk/cds/rd/ccdb.htm

De Bruijn, H. (2001) *Managing Performance in the Public Sector.* London: Routledge.

De Gues, A. (1997) *The Living Company: Habits for survival in a turbulent business environment.* Boston: Harvard Business School Press.

Demos (2003) *Inside Out: Rethinking Inclusive Communities* http://www.demos.co.uk/uploadstore/docs/INCO_ft.pdf.

Denning, S. (2001)*The Springboard: How Storytelling Ignites Action in Knowledge-Era Organizations.* Oxford: Butterworth-Heinemann.

DFID (1997) *Eliminating world poverty: The challenge for the 21ˢᵗ century.* London: Stationery Office.

Diez Canseco, J., Alejos, W., Mena, M., Valdivia, J. and Franceza, K. (2002) *Informe Final: Comisión Investigadora de Delitos Económicos y Financieros 1990–2001.* Lima: Congreso de la República del Perú.

DiMaggio, P. J. and Powell, W. W. (1991) 'The Iron Cage Revisited: Institutional Isomorphism and Collective Rationality in Organisation Fields' in W. W. Powell & P. J. DiMaggio (eds.).

Dubois, D. (1993) *Competency-based Performance Improvement, A Strategy for Organizational Change.* Amherst MA: HRD Press.

Dubois D. (ed.) (1998) *The Competency Case Book.* Amherst MA: HRD Press.

Eade, D. and Ligteringen, E. (eds.) (2001) *Debating Development.* Oxford: Oxfam GB.

Edwards, M. and Hulme, D. (eds.) (1995) *Non-Governmental Organisations: Performance and accountability, beyond the magic bullet.* London: Save the Children and Earthscan.

Ellerman, D. (2001) 'Helping People to Help Themselves; towards a theory of autonomy-compatible development'. Washington: World Bank.

Engel, P., Carlsson, C. and Van Zee, A. (2003) *Making evaluation results count: Internalizing evidence by learning.* Maastricht: ECDPM Policy Management Brief, 16.

Escobar, A. (1995) *Encountering Development: The making and unmaking of the third world.* Chichester, West Sussex: Princeton University Press.

Estrella, M. et al. (eds.) (2000) *Learning From Change: Issues and experiences in participatory monitoring and evaluation.* London: ITDG.

Foucault, M. (1972) *The Archeology of Knowledge.* London: Routledge.

Fowler, A. (1992) 'Distant Obligations: Speculations on NGO Funding and the Global Market', *Review of African Political Economy*, 55: 9–29.

Fowler, A. (1997) *Striking a Balance: A Guide to Enhancing the Effectiveness of Non-Governmental Organisations in International Development.* London: Earthscan.

Friedland, R. and Alford, R. R. (1991), in W. W. Powell and P. J. DiMaggio (Eds.) *The New Institutionalism in Organizational Analysis.* London: University of Chicago Press.

Furtado, J. (2003) *Capacity Development Indicators for GEF Projects: Practical Guidance on their Design and Use by Key Actors.* Washington: Global Environment Facility, Internal Document.

Garratt, B. (2000), *The Twelve Organizational Capabilities: Valuing people at work.* London: Harpercollins Business.

Hailey, J. and Sorgenfrei, M (2004) 'Measuring Success: Issues in Performance Measurement'. Oxford: INTRAC, OPS No. 44.

Harrison, R. (1995) 'Steps towards the learning organisation' in *The collected papers of Roger Harrison.* London: McGraw Hill.

Hines, R. (1988) 'Financial accounting: In communicating reality we construct reality'. *Accounting, Organizations and Society*, 13 (3): 251–61.

Hodgkinson, G. and Sparrow, P. (2002) *The Competent Organization: A psychological analysis of the strategic management process.* Buckingham: Open University Press.

Horton, D. et al. (2003) *Evaluating Capacity Development.* The Hague: The International Service for National Agricultural Research.

Huddock, A. (1996) 'Sustaining Southern NGOs in Resource Dependent Environments'. *Journal of International Development*, 7 (4): 653–68.

Hulme, D. (2003) *Thinking 'small' and the understanding of poverty: Maymana and Mofizul's story.* Manchester: IDPM Working Paper No. 22.

Hulme, D. and Edwards, M. (1997) *NGOs, States and Donors: too close for comfort?* Hampshire and London: Save the Children and MacMillan.

INTRAC (2003) *Strengthening Civil Society: through research, practice and participation.* Promotional material. Oxford: INTRAC.

Ittner, C. and Larcker, D. (2003) 'Coming up Short on Nonfinancial Performance Measurement'. *Harvard Business Review*, November.

Jenster, P. and Hussey, D. (2001) *Company Analysis: Determining Strategic Capability*. Chichester: John Wiley.

Jepperson, R. L. (1991) 'Institutions, Instituional Effects and Institutionalism' in Powell and DiMaggio (eds.).

Johnson, H. T. (1999) 'Moving Upstream From Measurement' in P. Senge et al. *The Dance of Change; A Fifth Discipline Resource*. London: Nicholas Brealey.

Kaplan, A. (2001) 'Understanding development as a living process' in D. Lewis and T. Wallace (eds.) *Development NGOs and the Challenge of Change*. Connecticut: Kumarian Press.

Kerr, S. (2003) 'The Best-laid Incentive Plans'. *Harvard Business Review*, January.

Knights, D. and Willmott, H. C. (1985) 'Power and identity in theory and practice', *Sociological Review*, 33 (1): 22–46.

Lavergne, R., Lewis, E. and Pecore-Ugorji, D. (2004) *Capacity Development in CIDA's Bilateral Programming: A Stocktaking*. Quebec: CIDA internal document.

Letts, C., Ryan, W. and Grossman, A. (1999) *High Performance Nonprofit Organizations: Managing Upstream for Greater Impact*. New York: John Wiley.

Lindenberg, M. and Bryant, C. (2002) *Going Global: transforming relief and development NGOs*. Connecticut: Kumarian Press.

Lounsbury, M. (2003) 'The Problem of Order Revisited: towards a more critical institutional perspective' in R. Westwood and S. Clegg (eds.) *Debating Organization: Point – counterpoint in organization studies*. Oxford: Blackwell.

Lynch, R., Diezemann, J. and Dowling, J. (2003) *The Capable Company*. Oxford: Blackwell.

MacIntyre, A. (2002) *After virtue: A Study in Moral Theory*. London: Gerald Duckworth

Marsden, D. (1994) 'Indigenous Management and the Management of Indigenous Knowledge' in Wright S. (ed.) *Anthropology of Organisations*. London: Routledge.

Marsden, D., Oakley, P. and Pratt, B. (eds.) (1994) *Measuring the Process: Guidelines for Evaluating Social Development*. Oxford: INTRAC.

Marsden, D., Pratt, B. and Clayton, A. (eds.) (1998) *Outcomes and Impact: Evaluating Change in Social Development*. Oxford: INTRAC.

Mawdsley, E., Townsend, J., Porter,G. and Oakley, P. (2002) *Knowledge, Power and Development Agendas*. Oxford: INTRAC.

Mebrahtu, E. (2004) *Putting Policy into Practice: Participatory Monitoring and Evaluation in Ethiopia*. Oxford: INTRAC.

Meier, D. (2002) *In Schools We Trust: Creating Communities of Learning In An Era of Testing and Standardization*. Boston MA: Beacon Press.

Meyer, J. W. and Rowan, B. ([1977] 1991) 'Institutionalised Organisations: Formal structure as myth and ceremony' in Powell and DiMaggio (eds.).

Mintzberg, H. (1996) 'Managing Government: Governing Management'. *Harvard Business Review*, May.

Mizrahi, Y. (2003) *Capacity Enhancement Indicators: Review of the Literature*, WBI Evaluation Studies EG03–72. Washington: World Bank Institute.

Morgan, G. (1997) *Images of Organization*. London: Sage.

Munro, R. (1996) 'Alignment and Identity Work: the study of accounts and accountability' in R. Munro and J. Mouritsen (eds.) *Accountability: power, ethos and the technologies of managing*. London: International Thomson Business Press.

Neely, A. (2003) *Gazing into the Crystal Ball: The Future of Performance Measurement*, draft mimeo. Cranfield School of Management: Centre for Business Performance.

Neely, A. and Bourne, M. (n.d.) *Why Measurement Initiatives Fail*, draft mimeo. Cranfield School of Management: Centre for Business Performance.

Oakley, P. (ed.) (2001) *Evaluating Empowerment: Reviewing the Concept and Practice*. Oxford: INTRAC.

O'Neill, O. (2002) BBC Reith lectures www.bbc.co.uk/radio4

Perrin, B. (1998) 'Effective Use and Misuse of Performance Measurement'. *American Journal of Evaluation*, 19 (3).

Powell, W. W. and DiMaggio, P. J. (eds.) (1991) *The New Institutionalism in Organizational Analysis*. London: University of Chicago Press.

Power, M. (1997) *The Audit Society: rituals of verification*. Oxford: Oxford University Press.

Pratt, B. (2002) *People and Change: Exploring Capacity-Building in NGOs*. NGO Management and Policy Series 15. Oxford: INTRAC.

Randell, J., German, T. and Ewing, D. (2002) *The Reality of Aid: An Independent Review of Development Cooperation*. London: Earthscan.

Rihani, S. (2001) *Complex Systems Theory and Development Practice: Understanding non-linear realities*. London: Zed Press.

Ritzer, G. (1996) *The McDonaldization of Society*. Thousand Oaks, California: Pine Forge.

Rondinelli, D. (1993) *Development Projects as Policy Experiments: An Adaptive Approach to Development Administration*. London: Routledge.

Roper, L., Pettit, J. and Eade, D. (2003) *Development and the Learning Organization*. Oxford: Oxfam.

Salaman, G. and Asch, D. (2003) *Strategy and Capability: Sustaining Organizational Change*. Oxford: Blackwell.

Sanchez, R. (ed.) (2001) *Knowledge Management and Organizational Competence*. Oxford: Oxford University Press.

Schön, D. (1983) *The Reflective Practitioner: How Professionals Think in Action*. Hampshire, UK: Avebury Press.

Scott, J. (1997) *Moral Economy of the Peasant: Rebellion and Subsistence in South East Asia*. New Haven: Yale University Press.

Scott, J. (1998) *Seeing Like a State: How Certain Schemes to Improve the Human Condition Have Failed*. New Haven: Yale University Press.

Scott, R. W. (1987) 'The adolescence of institutional theory'. *Adminstrative Science Quarterly* 32 (4): 493–511.

Scott-Villiers, P. (2002) 'The struggle for organisational change: how the ActionAid Accountability, Learning and Planning System emerged'. *Development and Practice* 12 (3&4): 424–35.

Sen, A. (1999) *Development as Freedom*. New York: Alfred A. Knopf.

Senge, P. (1990) *The Fifth Discipline*. New York: Doubleday Currency.

Senge, P., Kleiner, A., Roberts, C., Ross, R., Roth, G. and Smith, B. (1999) *The Dance of Change; A Fifth Discipline Resource*. London: Nicholas Brealey.

Shein, E. (1999) *Process Consultation Revisited: Building the Helping Relationship*. Boston: Addison Wesley.

Somerville, I. and Mroz, J. (1997) 'New Competencies for a New World' in Hesselbein, F., Goldsmith M. and Beckhard R. (eds.). *The Organization of the Future*. San Francisco: Jossey-Bass.

Stiglitz, J. (2002) *Globalization and its Discontents*. London: Penguin Books.

Stiles, K. (ed.) (2000) *Global Institutions and Local Empowerment: Compiling theoretical perspectives*. London: Macmillan.

Strathern, M. (2001) *Audit Culture: Anthropological studies in accountability, ethics and the academy*. London: Routledge.

Taylor, J. (2000) *So now they are going to measure empowerment!* Community Development Resource Association. www.cdra.org.za

Taylor J. (2003) *Organizations and Development: Towards building a practice.* Cape Town: CDRA.

Tevoedjre, A. (2002) *Winning the war against humiliation.* Report of the independent commission on Africa and the challenges of the third millennium. New York: UNDP.

Thin, N. (2002) *Social Progress and Sustainable Development.* London: ITDG Publishing.

UNAIDS/WHO (2002) *AIDS Epidemic Update.*

UNCTAD (2000) *Aid, Private Capital Flows and External Debt: The Challenge of Financing Development in the Least Developed Countries.* New York: United Nations.

UNDP (2001) *Human Development Report. Making new technologies work for human development.*

Wallace, T. and Chapman, J. (2002) *The donor landscape for UK development NGOs.* Draft Paper prepared for ISTR Conference, July 2002, Cape Town, South Africa.

Wallace, T., Crowther, S. and Shepherd, A. (1997) *Standardising development: Influences on UK NGOs' policies and procedures.* Oxford: Worldview Press.

Wenger, E. (1998) *Communities of Practice.* Cambridge: Cambridge University Press.

Wenger, E., McDermott, R. and Snyder, W. (2002) *Cultivating Communities of Practice. A Guide to Managing Knowledge.* Boston: Harvard Business School Press.

Wheatley, M. and Kellner-Rogers, M. (1996) *A Simpler Way.* San Francisco: Berrett-Koehler.

Willmott, H. (1996) 'Thinking Accountability: accounting for the disciplined production of the self' in R. Munro & J. Mouritsen (eds.) *Accountability: power, ethos and the technologies of managing.* London: International Thomson Business Press.

Wright, S. (ed.) (1994) *Anthropology of Organisations.* London: Routledge.

Yeung, A., Ulrich, D., Nason, S. and Von Glinow, M. (1999) *Organizational Learning Capability: Generating and Generalizing Ideas with Impact.* Oxford: Oxford University Press.

Appendix

A Review of INTRAC's International Conferences on the Evaluation of Social Development

International workshops on the evaluation of social development have been a regular feature of the INTRAC calendar for nearly fifteen years. The first of these events was held in Swansea in 1989, when eighty people came together to examine the concept of social development itself and implications for its evaluation. During proceedings, discussion revolved around four key issues: (1) qualitative indicators, (2) issues of methodology, (3) the role of the evaluator, and (4) partnership. Out of the debates came the realisation that evaluation has two distinct origins, manifested on the one hand in a scientific or technocratic approach to society and development, and on the other, a more relativist or interpretative approach. Key conclusions of the workshop included an understanding of the importance of regarding evaluation as a learning exercise, and of having regard for the cultural context within which evaluation takes place. Further lessons included the need to be questioning of the style of an evaluation, the use of external consultants and their qualification and appropriateness for the task. Predetermined or blueprint approaches were considered by most to be, at the best, problematic. The proceedings were published by Oxfam under the title *Evaluating Social Development Projects.*[1]

The second conference, held in the Netherlands in 1992, was a smaller affair, involving around 35 participants, who were seeking to relate some of the ideas of the earlier conference to their practical application. Drawing from their own experience, the participants produced guidelines for evaluating social development, working from a framework that covered (1) preparation, (2) execution and (3) analysis and reflection. Issues that arose out of discussion during the conference focused around the problem of real time and costs, especially for NGOs and the imbalance between quantitative and qualitative approaches. It was noted that there was, in general, a reluctance to let the evaluation process run without attempts to regulate it by imposing procedural straightjackets or frameworks. The gap between theoretical commitment and operational practice was also noted. These debates and findings were summarised in an INTRAC publication, *Measuring the Process: Guidelines for Evaluating Social Development.*[2]

---

[1] Marsden, D. and Oakley, P. (1990) *Evaluating Social Development Projects*. Oxford: Oxfam.

[2] Marsden, D., Oakley, P. and Pratt, B. (1994) *Measuring the Process*, Oxford: INTRAC.

In 1996, a third conference was held, again in the Netherlands, that looked specifically at some of the issues around the assessment of impact and outcomes of social development programmes. The conference centred around the presentation of some forty case studies, so as to facilitate an exploration of the gap between strong rhetoric on impact assessment and the reality of weaker practice. Revisiting the concept of social development, there was a general consensus that it is linked to a vision of greater social justice and access to public resources. For most participants, social change and transformation are the essential dynamic of social development. Lessons from practice were summarised and published by INTRAC in 1998 under the title: *Outcomes and Impact: Evaluating Change in Social Development.*[3]

All these conferences were attended, in more or less equal numbers, by participants from Northern and Southern development agencies (the latter mainly from NGOs, the former from both NGOs and official agencies). However, at the end of the third conference, it was felt that follow-up work should branch off in two different directions. First, prior to the Fourth Evaluation Conference it was planned that four regional workshops should be held so as to increase the numbers of people involved in the debate. In the end, the initial workshops in Bangladesh, Jordan, Tanzania and Nicaragua were followed by further events in Peru, Sri Lanka, Indonesia and Sweden. Second, more action research needed to be carried out into experimentation with different monitoring and evaluation methods. Oxfam and ActionAid/Novib undertook this work, the results of which have subsequently been published.

The Fourth Conference, held in Oxford in 2000, was able to build upon these regional workshops as well as draw from a series of important commissioned papers and the experiences of the one hundred participants present. A significant and widely-held conclusion of the conference was that the debate about the relative strengths and weaknesses of qualitative and quantitative approaches is essentially fruitless. It was felt that no more time need be wasted on weighing up these approaches, as both are important and impact cannot be gauged without qualitative input from clients/beneficiaries. There was also a general realisation that the evaluation of empowerment can, as an activity in itself, be either disempowering or empowering. As such, the need to be fully aware of the implications and effects of approaches and models was emphasised. Finally, a number of participants noted that many of the newer approaches to development can only work if power structures and relationships within society are fully understood and taken into account. The papers from this conference were published by INTRAC in 2001 in the volume, *Evaluating Empowerment: Reviewing the Concept and Practice.*[4]

---

[3] Oakley, P., Pratt, B. and Clayton, A. (1998) *Outcomes and Impact.* Oxford: INTRAC.

[4] Oakley, P. (2001) *Evaluating Empowerment.* Oxford: INTRAC.

Index

Fourth Conference on the Evaluation of Social Development (INTRAC) 168